bold, gutsy, brazen, *outrageous*, audaciou

courageous, in-your-face, strong, adventurous, estroge

fueled, powerful, proud, brave, unabashed, sma

precocious, muckraker, full of chutzpah, valiant, hero

daring, fearless, **PLUCKY**, forward, intuitiv

empowered, unblushing, proud, self-assured, se

possessed, self-confident, full of oneself, spirited, playf

feisty, gorgeous, irresistible, *sensual*, sex

shameless, **CONTROVERSIAL**, challenging, belligere

bigheaded, hotheaded, excessive, bossy, brash, brat

bitchy, tenacious, stick-to-itive-ness, compassiona

CONCERNED, righteous, loving, inspiring, creativ

engaging, competent, capable, able, effective, successf

great, glorious, fabulous, influential, ascendant, geni

goddess, supreme, superior, ***all-powerful,*** more th

a match for, having teeth, in force, in full force, in f

effect, in full swing, woman-on-top, lusty, red-hot mam

immodest, SHAMELESS HUSSY, vulg

ocking, scandalizing, mighty, vigorous, souped-up,

ud, shout, CROW, brag, boast, show off, swagger,

ot your own horn, booming, forceful, formidable,

mpelling, not to be trifled with, high-powered, high-

eared, barefaced, **thick-skinned,** up to no good,

ettlesome, naughty, cheeky, sassy, inappropriate,

rident, brassy, arrogant, impudent, overwhelming,

ncontestable, victorious, unbeaten, sovereign,

nceasing, undiminished, refreshed, in fine feather, in

p form, a leader, strong-armed, urgent, pressing,

nphatic, assertive, **ROCK HARD,** hard as

on, tough as steel, steely, bold as brass, adamant,

inforced, toughened, deep-rooted, firm, solid,

bstantial, stable, fixed, well-built, stout, **STRONG**

S A HORSE, strong as a lion, strong as an ox,

ady, undiluted, undiminished, whole, strengthened,

rtified, double-strength, entrenched, unassailable,

nmixed, durable, enduring, large, heavy, weighty, huge,

That Takes Ovaries!

That Takes Ovaries!

bold females and their brazen acts

EDITED BY

Rivka Solomon

 THREE RIVERS PRESS
NEW YORK

Published by Three Rivers Press, New York, New York.
Member of the Crown Publishing Group, a division of Random House, Inc.

www.randomhouse.com

THREE RIVERS PRESS is a registered trademark and the Three Rivers
Press colophon is a trademark of Random House, Inc.

Printed in the United States of America

DESIGN BY ELINA D. NUDELMAN

Library of Congress Cataloging-in-Publication Data

That takes ovaries!: bold females and their brazen acts/edited by Rivka
    Solomon.—1st ed.

    1. Women—Biography. 2. Women—Conduct of life. 3. Courage.
    4. Risk-taking (Psychology) I. Solomon, Rivka.

    HQ1123.A3 T53 2002

    305.4'092'2—dc21   2001053507

ISBN 0-609-80659-9

10 9 8 7 6 5 4

First Edition

Dedicated to girls everywhere,
and to those fighting for the human rights of
women and girls around the globe.

Contents

CHAPTER 2

After Some Thought: Making Life-changing Choices 50

CHAPTER 3

For Ourselves: Taking Charge of Our Bodies and Sexuality 70

CHAPTER 6

Doing It Together: Collective Activism

CHAPTER 7

"That's Not Nice!": Acting On Anger

"If you obey all the rules, you miss all the fun."

–*Katharine Hepburn*

"Well-behaved women rarely make history."

–*Laurel Thatcher Ulrich*

"If you don't take risks, you won't know what is possible."

–*Unknown*

oversized, big for one's age, thick, thick-ribbed, barrel-chested, **broad-shouldered,** broad-shouldered, stout, timbered, of good constitution, robust, hardy, dense, indivisible, unbreakable, indestructible, shatterproof, strong-fibered, tasty, flavorful, **SPICY,** spicy, racy, full-flavored, full-bodied, generous, well-matured, young for one's age, penetrating, intense, deep, self-respecting, **EXPRESSIVE,** meaningful, informative, striking, vivid, highly colored, making no bones about it, frank, blunt, blatant, outspoken, strongly worded, upfront, straight from the hip, *not afraid to be different,* not afraid to be difficult, loudmouthed, bigmouthed, smart-mouthed, cheeky, give lip, get under one's collar, get under one's skin, thumb one's nose at, stick one's tongue out, give the finger, ruffle, **BE INSOLENT,** irritate, sow the seeds of discontent, cause discontent, look for trouble, stir up trouble, make trouble, ask for it, mix it up, **be spoiling for a fight,** make something of it

DEFIANT, having gumption, taking no guff, ...tivist, agitator, against the grain, incite, inspire, up the ...te, double the stakes, look big, ***throw out* *...nes's chest,** beat one's chest, show a bold front, ...ave a banner, brandish, march, demonstrate, not be ...oved, challenge, dissent, oppose, not take it lying down, ...and up for one's beliefs, stand up for one's rights, refuse ... bow down, ask for trouble, **CONFRONT,** be ...tive, irreverent, unconventional, assert oneself, be up in ...ms, REACT, resist, not do as one is told, disobey ...ders, show insubordination, be a renegade, challenge, ...fy the whip, disrupt, rebel, come out, agitate, protest, ...ck ass, ***kick up a ruckus,*** raise a stink, stage a ...volt, lead a rebellion, rise up, be free, throw off the yoke, ...row off the shackles, fight for independence, overthrow, ...**evolutionize,** full of courage, full of ...ght, full of spirit, full of beans, spunky, impressive, ...nergetic, active, vibrant, dynamic, rocking, industrious,

Introduction

What Is This Book?

That Takes Ovaries! is a collection of women's and girls' real-life stories written in their own words. From courageous and smart to outrageous and foolhardy, these accounts capture the breadth of gutsy acts. It is a collection that embraces diversity with the voices of everyday females of many ages and cultural backgrounds, and also includes stories from a few better-known individuals and activists.

This book contains more than sixty first-person narratives representing a wide variety of audacious deeds. It includes accounts of women and girls standing up to a gun-toting gang-banger in a fast-food joint, skysurfing out of airplanes, organizing a hundred high-school girls to take on the boys who harass them, jumping off a moving train to see the Alps, defying abuse in prison, diving into the middle of an ice hockey fight, staging a Lesbian Avengers action inside a conservative think tank, earning a living as a sex writer, making a would-be burglar cry, and telling President Clinton what to do—and having him do it! The stories tell how a fourteen-year-old led a revolt in her synagogue, a poor woman rose out of destitution and prostitution, a passerby confronted a crowd of catcalling men, a public health educator founded the country's first women-oriented sex-toy store, a peacemaker met with guerilla leaders in a war zone, a girl was the first to wear pants to elementary school in the

1960s, a reporter started a mass movement against brutality toward women in the Middle East, a Catholic schoolteacher snuck in to see the Pope . . . and dozens of other sassy, spirited acts.

That Takes Ovaries! places all its stories, from the seemingly frivolous to the obviously political, under the single umbrella of a larger philosophy: freedom and empowerment. What's the link between the woman who boldly fights for social justice and the one who boldly has fun? Both are acting powerfully, because each is rejecting preconceived notions of how females "should" behave. Each storyteller is irreverently saying, "No way I'm accepting limits placed on me!"

How Did This Book Come About?

I had a party one night. The guests were more acquaintances than good friends. During the evening a man told a story about a woman who had done a totally brazen thing (though now I can't remember what). When he finished, I casually remarked, "Well, that took ovaries." The roomful of people fell silent, and then they burst out laughing, exclaiming "Great phrase!" I was surprised. I'd used the saying often enough in the past, around my buddies, and gotten back only nods, grins, or "Amen to that." This time, using the expression with the general public, I saw its power.

This phrase is *great,* I thought after my guests left. Not just fun and funny, it challenged the myth of the passive female—and that made it political. Even more, the phrase reflected a key sentiment behind the latest rising wave of young feminists (the Guerilla Girls, Riot Grrrl, Third Wave, and girls' movements), that is, the attitude of playful brazenness in the push for gender equality.

Besides all that, I concluded as I flossed before bed, "that takes ovaries" would make a great book title!

By the time I climbed under the covers, I had decided to assemble a collection of ovarian acts where women and girls take charge, and maybe even have fun. I hoped my book-to-be could add to those already coming out that are a platform for girls' vibrant voices and a celebration of womanly resilience. I envisioned a book that would excite women and men of all ages who want to see their sisters, mothers, grandmothers, aunts, and friends leading empowered lives; mothers and fathers who care about their daughters growing up self-assured and confident; and girls eager to be a part of the growing "girl power" movement. *That Takes Ovaries!* would be for everyone interested in challenging a culture still wrought with inequality and double standards—everyone hungry for unabashedly powerful females.

Collecting the Stories

The day after my party I whipped up a "call for stories." I e-mailed the notice to friends and a few listservs (e-mail discussion groups).

That Takes Ovaries!

Seeking submissions of anything YOU have *ever* done—little or big—that was gutsy or audacious. It can be playful, serious, spontaneous, calculated, smart, sexy, and/or an example of leadership. Something that when you think about it today, makes you nod your head with *pride,* or even semi-disbelief, and think, "Wow! I did that!"

Soon my e-mail in-box was full. Not only with cool, gutsy-gal submissions, but also with notes from women and men around the country saying they loved the idea of the book and asking when they could buy it. Apparently the phrase had struck a

3

chord. When women got the e-notice, they were so tickled they promptly sent it to their girlfriends; my call for stories became a popular forwarding item. Before long I was seeing it *sent back to me* via a number of women's listservs and e-newsletters to which I subscribed but had not sent the notice. In the end, three hundred stories came in and thousands of women on the Web considered, at least for a moment, their own bravery and brazenness.

Defining Ovaries

What does it mean to *have ovaries?* If I was going to edit this book, I'd need a definition.

First, I tried to define the male equivalent: *having balls. That takes balls,* I surmised, is what you say about a man who has done something rather fearless, a guy we might envy for having the confidence to push the boundaries or break the rules. Actually, I thought, these were great characteristics for *any* person to have . . . but they'd be especially helpful to a woman. She'd need just these traits to live fully in a world that often tries to limit her. So even as I kept an open mind regarding defining *ovaries,* I also kept this *balls* description in the back of my head. Then I set about reading the stories. With each one, I gained a clearer picture of what *other* women thought the expression *that takes ovaries* meant. I merged the contributors' ideas with my own until I reached a working definition.

Something *takes ovaries,* I concluded, when it is *bold, gutsy, brazen, outrageous, audacious, courageous,* or *in-your-face*. Combined, this string of words encompasses the spectrum of what *having ovaries* is about. (For more ovarian synonyms, see the beginning of this book. Just reading it, your inner bite-me grrl grows stronger.) *Having ovaries* is a catchall phrase. It includes smart, brave, altruistic acts and silly, shocking, impulsive ones. So, it seems, having ovaries isn't that far from the definition of having balls—except that we are female.

By adapting the phrase *that takes balls* to *that takes ovaries,* we end the myth that equates only the male sex organ with innate power and fearlessness. By adapting the phrase, we claim our inherent strength and courage, too. Hell, we've been acting on our strength all along; the only new thing is that now we have a cool expression we can use to brag about it.

The predominant culture may try to socialize girls into believing femaleness and femininity equals not-as-powerful, not-as-bold. (Even common put-downs targeted at guys who act less than macho instill this idea: *You have no balls; Don't be such a girl;* and plain old *pussy*—simultaneously the slang for female genitalia and an insult.) It's so pervasive, no wonder some girls have to fight to keep from internalizing the notion that being female means being *less than.*

But the stories I collected show women and girls *are* actively fighting this view of themselves. In fact, the stories illustrate that for many contributors to this book, *having ovaries* specifically means having the courage to confront externally defined notions of what a woman is. Many of the stories are about defying the dominant culture's preconceived idea of "femininity"— passive, pleasing, docile, cautious, dependent, either quiet or hysterical, irrational, dumb, always-nice-never-angry, and incapable of self-defense. Yes, women can be those things, too. After all, we are human and reserve our right to be hysterical when we want (so there!). But the stories in this book show that females—the beings who personify *real* femininity—are more than what others tell them they are. They are loudly and proudly whoever and whatever they want to be.

In that same vein, coining the phrase *having ovaries* doesn't mean women aim to mimic men who *have balls.* In fact, this would be difficult to achieve even if they wanted to. Everything happens within a context, and ours is a culture that imposes different roles and conditioning on boys than on girls. When trained-to-be-confident men, who already hold much of the power in society, act "overconfident" or "reckless" (connotations of *ballsy*), some onlookers may feel a tinge of trepidation and think, "This could be a scary thing." When trained-to-be-cautious women act "overconfident," yes, it could be a scary thing, too, but more likely it would be a breath of fresh air, as in: "Ah, finally, a woman who feels she has an equal right to be in charge." And if a woman acts "reckless," it would probably be along the lines of breaking the rules that have kept her down for millennia—like the conditioning that stops her from fighting back when assaulted.

Even in a quest to be an assertive Woman of Ovaries, it is unlikely a woman would permanently give up her loving, gentle side, even if she abandons it temporarily. Certainly, losing this side would be undesirable. But be warned—and get ready to cheer!—because some of the women in this book do indeed temporarily abandon their niceness.

An additional note regarding defining *ovaries:* In the context of this book, *having ovaries* isn't about possessing certain sex organs or chromosomes. It's about being female-identified and possessing a certain Attitude (with a capital *A*). All types of women and girls are welcome here, including females born without ovaries, those who've had ovaries removed, those who acquired new plumbing via medical intervention, and intersexed and transgendered folk who identify, or who have ever identified, as women.

A final comment on terms: When I use "women and girls" and "we" in this book, I do so fully aware and appreciative of both the differences and similarities present in the vast group of people who identify as female. Women's cultural diversity is to be treasured, and uniformity is not the goal. However, building coalitions amid female diversity and acknowledging commonality makes women more effective in organizing for mutual interests: chief among them, that every woman and girl be free to live her life to her fullest potential.

Multiple Messages

Meanwhile each female is a unique individual, and not all females receive the same socialization. Only by listening to one another's experiences and stories do we learn about the multiple messages each girl gets about how a female "should" act in her particular family and racial, cultural, or economic community. Only then do we understand the complexity of how each community teaches its females to be strong in certain ways but to acquiesce in others. A girl may be encouraged to be opinionated . . . until a guy walks into the room. Or perhaps she's raised to be powerful . . . yet tolerant of her boyfriend's hitting her. Maybe she is taught by her community to be defiant . . . but to put up with things that an empowered woman surely wouldn't—from smiling (instead of talking back) when harassed to stifling dreams and desires to not being proud of who she is.

Even if a girl is raised by her family to be assertive, as soon as she steps out the door, or turns on the TV, she is bombarded with the mainstream's definition of femininity. Besides the fact that it's hard to resist the predominant culture, a girl could be punished for trying. Her assertiveness, though encouraged at home, might be labeled "loud, aggressive, bitchy" once outside.

And there is one thing many subcultures and the dominant culture have in common: a tolerance of high levels of physical and sexual abuse against women. Most cultures view as normal a variety of offenses, from women being afraid to walk alone at night to a media industry that makes a fortune turning sexual harassment and sexual violence into entertainment.

So although different cultural groups' messages may dominate at different times, in the end most girls are repeatedly told to tolerate a devaluing of themselves.

Good thing so many girls don't do as they're told!

Who Are the Contributors?

There are so many ways to be female—and this book embraces them. The contributors identify (sometimes in their stories, sometimes not) as African-American, Asian-American, Caucasian, Jewish, Latina, Middle Eastern, Native American, bilingual, bicultural, mixed race, heterosexual, bisexual, lesbian, working-class, middle-class, and upper-class, mother, childless, single, coupled, polyamorous, able-bodied, living with a disability, child, teen, adult, and elder. Most are from the United States, but this book also includes contributors from Africa, Asia, Europe, Latin America, and the Middle East. A third of them are professional writers, folks who carefully crafted their submissions. But the majority are not. Many got the "call for stories" electronically forwarded from a pal and then hastily e-mailed their true tales to me on what I'd call a *well-thought-out whim*. Their narratives included much of the informality that comes with the medium of e-mail, and the wholesome rawness found in unpolished, authentic experience. It was both a pleasure and a challenge to edit them.

The stories in this book are dramatically written but true. All dialogue and description are recounted to the best of the writer's recollection. To protect the innocent, and guilty, a few changed their own or others' names.

Many of the contributors' stories are about women and girls taking command of a situation. A number are model-citizen or social justice acts that others might like to emulate. But I would not encourage the reader to undertake all the deeds detailed here. In fact, not every contributor to this book would necessarily condone all the acts in it. Likely, some contributors, and some readers, will disapprove of the audacious, sexual, or acting-on-anger stories. And why shouldn't they? Women are not a monolithic group. They are diverse, with diverse opinions, values, and aspirations.

Yet, at the same time, I'll bet the acts not seen initially as role-model material will still be considered models of a sort by some.

Though the contributor might not encourage others to replicate her particular deed, readers might find themselves cheering her on nonetheless. After all, she has the nerve to walk through her fear, the gumption to go outside her own self-imposed limits, and the confidence to reject our culture's restrictive notions of what a female can do. She is taking action.

On the other hand, some readers may feel she has crossed the line. But the book is supposed to be about that, too: women and girls being a little impulsive and crazy—a little Thelma and Louise-ish. So some of the contributors are wild and impetuous. They abandon common sense, civility, or caution as they stand up for themselves, defend loved ones (or strangers), express anger, or risk their lives for a dream, a political statement, or plain ole fun. Well, who says you don't need ovaries for those things, too?

Men: A Pro-Partnership Philosophy

There were two possible ways to introduce the three hundred stories I received for this book: One, ignore the fact that two-thirds were tales of women standing up to men trying to hurt them. Two, acknowledge it.

In short, when asked, "Hey, what have *you* ever done that was bold, gutsy, or brazen?," many women answered loud and clear: "I fought back."

There were fathers who battered, boyfriends who raped, and strangers who catcalled, groped, used guns, fists, or date-rape drugs. The list goes on. Reading the submissions, I was floored. So much assault.

Obviously these stories are not just isolated instances. This pattern is a larger social problem, happening within a wider political context. Some call it *patriarchy*. Your grandma might have called it "a man's world." Whatever we've labeled it over the years, the reality is that it hurts women. The evidence:

Women are still struggling for the right to live without violence, have equal representation in their political institutions, and receive equal pay for their work.

Does this mean men are the enemy?

No.

Most women love, adore, hug, hold, birth, help raise, build homes and snowmen, eat pancakes and sushi, create babies and sidewalk murals, debate prison reform and the international space station, and/or happily sex it up with males every day. The world is full of good men.

But this does not mean we should keep quiet about how women and girls worldwide must defend themselves against violence or the threat of violence on a regular basis. Sharing personal experiences aloud can be the foundation for any political movement. For any society to evolve, for any people to be free, before reality on the ground can be changed, the truth needs to be told. *Truth:* The FBI estimates that on average a woman is raped every six minutes in the United States (and those are only the reported rapes). *Truth:* Every fourteen seconds a woman is physically assaulted in the United States. *Truth:* One of every three women in the world has been beaten, coerced into sex, or otherwise abused in her lifetime.

But women are not alone. In fact, women and girls have natural partners in their truth-telling task: men and boys. The institution of patriarchy hurts them as well. They, too, are on the receiving end of male violence. They, too, need to break the taboo against telling the truth about their lives.

Boys are born loving, caring, cooperative. Those who become men-who-hurt don't do so all on their own. A substantial number have witnessed or were themselves victims of beatings and sexual abuse. Even more widespread, however, is the systematic, often violent, squashing of boys by people who have already internalized hurtful social constructs of "masculinity." Our society's warped norms instruct boys to fit their beautiful, sprawling humanity into an itty-bitty box of what a man is "supposed" to be: strong to the point of being stoic; hard to the point of being emotionally numb; and, yes, sometimes powerful to the point of being oppressive. There is little room in that box for any human expressions deemed "girlish"—such as sadness, tenderness, vulnerability, and nurturing—even though those are just the sentiments that could help heal the negative effects of all the squashing.

Of course, internalizing rigid ideals of manhood or experiencing systematic violence does not negate personal responsibility for violent behavior toward others. It just makes it easier to understand its origin. Whatever the origin, everyone must try to stop the violence targeted at *any* of us. And women who publicly talk about the courage it took to stand up against assault are doing just that. By speaking out, they not only create momentum for political action to end the violence, they also begin to liberate themselves in the process.

Women's and girls' liberation will not be complete, however, until it is widely understood how our culture of institutionalized sexism hurts everyone. How it tries to turn inherently strong girls into women who hesitate to use their power (even in self-defense), and inherently compassionate boys into men with an inclination to dominate. Gender straitjackets. For any one group to be free, everyone needs to be free; no one should be stopped—not by stereotyping, not by violence—from expressing his or her full range of emotions and abilities. So, while this book includes women and girls telling the truth about their lives, I hope it also encourages men and boys, women's allies in our mutual liberation struggles, to do the same.

What Is the Main Point of This Book?

My hope is that the narratives here affirm the reader's already bold life—or expand her imagination of what is possible for herself and her society. I want girls and women to be empowered by seeing what others do.

From girlhood, many are trained to step lightly, carefully, even though being assertive, making noise, and creating waves are often the skills that help a girl most—whether advancing her career or ensuring her safety.

By celebrating bold, risk-taking women, I hope to encourage others to take risks. Struggle and risk are part of any attempt at personal or social change. Like courage, risk-taking is infectious. This is true both between people and within a person. Between, it is motivating to witness someone else's courage. Within, an individual develops confidence and experience by taking risks and living through them; the more risks she takes in one area of her life, the more she feels able to take them in others. She may start with a gutsy act for pleasure—instigating an erotic interlude with messy paints, tracking huge gorillas alone in West Africa, shaving hairy legs in playful stripes, tricking a pimp out of his money—and before long she won't put up with any timidity, any pussyfooting around in any area of her life.

Once a girl is initiated and passes the *I'm-a-risk-taker* threshold, and she knows she can act regardless of fear, her life becomes fuller. With newfound confidence, she is willing to address unfair treatment she experiences or witnesses. She is no longer able to tolerate the sight of injustice without trying to address it, *because she no longer feels it is beyond her ability to succeed.*

She'll run her sister's batterer out of town, bawl out a racist cop (even though she is only five years old!), spread her legs hundreds of times to teach doctors how to properly care for women's gynecological health, mount a pee protest in demand of wheelchair-accessible bathrooms on campus, and save a girl she doesn't know from being beaten on the side of the highway. If a woman lives her life in a more daring mode all the time, then there will be no question about whether she will stand up for herself and others when mistreated, and no question she'll fight back if attacked.

I want to recognize girls and women who are not afraid to act contrary to how the predominant norms say they should, not afraid to break the rules, act improperly, get dirty. All that is part of leading a "no limits" life. The main message of the book? *Enjoy being bold, and if that is scary at first, marvel at your ability to walk through fear.* Not letting fear stop us in one area of our lives means we are less likely to let it stop us in others, from defending ourselves against a single incident of discrimination to changing the world for the better.

Happy reading!
Rivka, 2002

Realizing You Have Ovaries

You may not know you have ovaries. Then all of a sudden you'll do something or say something and *Yowza*, it hits you: *I'm one strong mutha! It's an awakening.* Maybe you had no clue about your own ovaries, but admired those of others. Maybe you hoped you had it in you, but had never tried to tap into it. This realization of one's own strength and power can happen at any age. It is most exciting, though, when it happens to young ones. There is something about knowing a girl has eighty years of serious ass-kicking ahead of her that sends chills up the spine.

Always Knowing You Had Ovaries

You always knew you had ovaries. Always. You knew you were born with the power to stand up for your beliefs and say no to authority. And you've been exercising that power since day one, much to the consternation of your parents, teachers, and other disapproving (or is it jealous?) adults around you. But you knew better than to stop. You knew better than to ever squash down that part of you that is defiant and real.

Rivka's Note to All Readers*

Girls are born self-assured and bold.

It is not a chromosomal thing that makes many girls shy about speaking up in class, hesitant to dive into competitive sports, or tolerant of street harassment. It's not due to genetic makeup that women are less likely to run for political office, climb the corporate ladder, or attain equality—whether equal pay on the job or equal attention in the bedroom. It's not nature; it's nurture. Internalized social messages and conditioning by a sexist, often violent society are what contributes to any female's suppressing her naturally confident, daring self and replacing it with less risk taking, less space-taking behavior.

Well, it's time to deprogram.

It's time to reject all that keeps a woman quiet or unsure. Many girls are conditioned to downplay their abilities or needs so that no one else's feathers get ruffled. Most women are taught not to push for or promote their own self-interests. This antiquated behavior has kept women back.

What femininity needs is a boost of bravado.

We perk up and take note when we hear about acts of female adventure and courage. They are stories we grab onto and delight in with others *("Hey, did you hear about the woman who . . .")*. We fix on these magnetic mental images and they become models of

---

*To be read at all open mikes

15

how we, too, can be in our lives *("If she can do it, so can I!")*. So what we need are role models galore—down and dirty role models. They show what is possible. They show how to counteract the subtle and overt messages telling us to be "good girls" even when doing so isn't in our best interest.

Fortunately, role models abound. They are in every racial, cultural, and socioeconomic group, and in girls and women of every age, sexual orientation, ability, and disability. They are everywhere, because they are us. Many girls believe in their strength in spite of cultural conditioning. Women find ways to skirt around and overcome efforts to program them. Examples of resistance, bravery, and breaking-the-mold behavior can be found in every female.

If courage creates ripples, get ready to be hit by a wave.

That Takes Ovaries! is a celebration of ourselves—girls and women just like you and me, speaking in our own words about our own actions. This is a celebration of everyday feisty females, those who haven't made the history books or the cover of *Time* magazine but who *have* taken on the tired, false stereotype of the passive female. Their gutsy acts spur us to be risk-takers and heroines in our day-to-day lives. Then we, creating ripples ourselves, inspire them in return with our own daring deeds.

That takes balls are words of praise reserved for a man who has done something bold: a guy we might respect for his ability to push the boundaries or break the rules, a boy with chutzpah. Well, *move over, gentlemen, it's time for the ladies!*

Some women need *ovaries* simply to survive in this harsh world. Others need them in order to flourish. But wherever an individual may fall on that spectrum, it is almost certain she will need to be a *Woman of Ovaries* if she wants to right wrongs, fight the injustices that still plague our communities, and gain her own freedom. Freedom, after all, isn't simply about rejecting conditioning; in the end, it's about dismantling the sexist institutions that promote the conditioning. We gotta be risk-takers to do that.

Of course, *all* stories are welcome here, whether they are

about hell-raising social change or hell-raising fun. Either act can be a life-altering experience if a girl is tossing aside the rules of how a female is "supposed" to behave.

Although some of the *ovarian* acts described here may seem too risky to you (and, in retrospect, they may seem that way to some of the people who did them), remember that the deeds were done with a sassy sense of valor and adventure. Of course, some were also done out of panic and blind instinct, and some yielded unsuccessful results. The aim is not to showcase perfect women doing perfect, selfless acts—though we'll witness some of those here, too. The goal is to showcase *real* women. Sometimes we make smart, calculated decisions; sometimes we take foolhardy chances. Either way, *that takes ovaries!*

That Takes Ovaries!

CHAPTER 1

On the Spot:
Impulsive, Gutsy Acts

SPONTANEOUS

impromptu

ACTING ON THE SPUR OF THE MOMENT

Sometimes we have our wits about us and we think on our feet. Sometimes we act before we think—*Ready . . . fire . . . aim!* Sometimes we don't think at all.

In these stories, women and girls rush up the ladder, run the length of the diving board, and jump in. Only on the way down, when they've already committed to the act, do they consider if there is enough water in the pool. And if there isn't, well, they'll figure something out.

This chapter is about women's and girls' capacity to calculate a situation with keen speed and make on-the-spot decisions that open up new possibilities for them . . . or save their butts. Whatever the motivation—whether they see an opportunity and grab it, tossing caution (and consequence) to the wind; whether they're forced to react quickly in order to protect themselves and loved ones; whether they don't want to lose face, or they feel the need to prove something—for the women and girls in these stories, instinct just takes over and they follow their gut reactions. What are gut reactions, after all, if not a type of lightning-quick intelligence?

There are certainly benefits to acting on the spur of the moment. Not only is there no time for others to shame her out of her actions, but when something happens fast and a woman responds *rapido*, the nay-saying voice in her head, the "Oh, you're not supposed to do *that*" refrain, doesn't get to utter a single disapproving word. It doesn't have time to get in the way of her doing what her body and soul tell her they really want to do. When a woman wants something bad, and she wants it *now*, she doesn't let internal obstacles (sometimes her worst enemy) get in the way—not fear, not finger-wagging. And when the deed is done, when things are calm again, pride bursts forth and she feels good.

Hey, wouldja look at what I just did!

Of course, not all impulsive acts ring with smarts. Whatever. There's still a good story to tell when it's over.

Preaching to the Convicted

kathleen tarr

As I lay napping one lazy summer morning, a crashing sound jarred me awake. I got up to investigate. I opened the bedroom door, wearing only my short, pink, baby-tee nightshirt, and was immediately confronted with a man staring back at me. His hand was extended toward the other side of the door handle. I tensed up and said nothing. He did the same.

Of all panicked thoughts, my priority was, *I'm not wearing any underwear.*

"What are you doing in here?" I yelled, leaning slowly toward the man, fists balled at my side.

With the foot of space between us closing fast, he backed up. Luckily, he did not choose the alternative. I bellowed again, "How did you get in here?" He turned nervously and looked at the open window behind him.

The stack of games I kept piled under the window lay strewn

all over the hardwood floor. Playing chips and dice were scattered everywhere, even under the furniture. Near the window leaned a shovel, which the intruder had apparently used to pry the window open, breaking the latch.

"You broke my window?" I asked, obviously a rhetorical question. "What are you doing in here?"

"I'm just looking for some money," he answered meekly. He hesitated and then continued, "Do you have any?"

It was my turn to pause. Then my answer surprised even me: "I'm not going to pay you for breaking into my house."

The shock of hearing this statement come out of my mouth completely distracted me from the fear surging inside my body. But it didn't distract me from my primary concern, which remained *How the hell can I get ahold of some underwear?*

Burgle-Man stood silently, reflecting perhaps on our situation.

While keeping my eyes fixed on Burgle-Man, I scanned the apartment with my peripheral vision. I was searching for my keys, my second priority. I'd need them to unlock the double-bolted front door in order to get him out. That was when I noticed my poster of Martin Luther King Jr. on the wall. I knew I needed to keep talking, and now Martin came to my aid.

Burgle-Man was a slight African-American, probably in his early forties, the ideal demographic for the tactic I had in mind. "You would look Martin Luther King in the eye and continue to rob this house?" I yelled, pointing to the poster. "You would know that the residents of this home believe in the causes of Black people, and you would still try to steal from them?"

Burgle-Man was speechless.

"You would ask my Black self for money, knowing Dr. King was watching?" I continued to scan for the keys, and continued to silently panic about my naked bottom half. I wondered if he would notice if I left the room just for a second to put on some underwear. But I had to keep talking. Eyeing other posters and prints on my living room walls, I asked Burgle-Man, "You would look at these celebrations of Sojourner Truth and

Toussaint L'Ouverture and cavalierly ransack this home for mere dollars?"

Burgle-Man's chin began to quiver.

Where were those damn keys? I wondered.

When I started my diatribe on Steven Biko and "our African sisters and brothers who struggle," tears streamed from Burgle-Man's penitent eyes. He cried, "I'm gonna change my ways! I'm gonna change my ways!"

"It's alright, Brother," I told him softly. *Who did I ever call "Brother"?* "If you start doing the right thing today, that's what you'll get to hold onto for the rest of your life." *Whatever that meant.*

Burgle-Man dried his tears while I spun my head around, looking for my keys. Of course, what I really longed for, needed, and had to have was my underwear. I could visualize the cotton fabulousness balled up in my dresser drawer just waiting for me. I hadn't missed them so much since I'd messed in my pants in the second grade.

"What are you looking for?" he asked.

"My keys."

"There's a key in the back door," he offered.

"You cased my place?" I hollered, vaguely remembering knocks at my front and back doors minutes before the break-in. He must have seen the key through a window from the outside.

"I'm sorry." His chin started quivering again.

I grabbed the spare key from the back door (which led to the backyard) and used it to open my front door. "Okay, good-bye," I grimaced.

"Are you going to call the police?" Burgle-Man asked.

"No, just get out. And don't do this again."

"I won't," he assured me solemnly, and retreated down the front stairs.

I relocked the door and collapsed on my couch, my legs no better than rubber bands. I sat still for ten minutes, quietly looking at Martin, before I got up and hammered the window shut. But first I got dressed.

kathleen tarr is a published legal scholar, a lecturer, a member of the California State Bar, and one of few Harvard Law School graduates who focused her legal career on eradicating racism and other oppressions, all the while refusing payment from her clients. For several years after the break-in, she slept with a knife. Having put the knife aside, she still never sleeps without underwear.

∞

Alps-ward Bound
frezzia prodero

I was twenty-one and traveling around Europe by myself for one month. It was a source of pride for me that I paid for the whole trip with my own hard-earned money. No parental help whatsoever. While abroad, I was determined to see the Alps, so I set it up to stay with a host family in Switzerland and hopped on a train. I didn't know exactly where to get off, but I wasn't worried; I figured the ticket collector would tell me when I'd reached the right station by yelling something obvious, like, "Alps, next stop." (I know, I know, silly me.)

After an hour of watching stop after stop pass by, I started worrying and decided to ask. I found the ticket collector by the train door just as we were pulling out of a station. I didn't speak the language, so I asked in my native Spanish and he answered in choppy English.

"It was *this* stop," he said. "You just missed it." He pointed to the station's platform, which was now zipping past us. "You'll have to get off at the next stop, two hours away in Italy, and buy another ticket—"

"Another ticket?"

"—to take the next train back," the ticket collector said as he walked away from me and into the train car.

"When is the next train back?" I asked, feeling the alarm rising up my chest.

"Tomorrow."

"What?" I yelled. "I'm supposed to meet a host family back at the station we just passed *today*."

It wasn't just that. I had nowhere to stay in Italy; no arrangements had been made. And I had no extra money for another ticket, or for a hotel. Just the night before I'd slept in a train station, and believe me, I was not eager to repeat the experience. So, in a crazed state, feeling the train picking up speed, I followed after the ticket collector who was walking down the narrow aisle between the passenger seats.

"What should I do? What should I do?" I asked him.

A man sitting nearby saw me panicking and said, "Jump!" I spun around and looked at him. He was serious. Suddenly, other passengers joined in, all urging me to jump. Even grandmothers. I thought of my alternative and nodded yes. They grabbed my bags from the overhead compartment and helped me to the door. I opened it, saw the ground rushing by, and jumped.

Yes, of course I was scared. But for some bizarre reason, in my anxious state, the thought of breaking down and having my parents wire me money seemed much worse than ending up in a full-body cast.

The ticket collector must have been shocked. He, or someone, pulled the emergency stop. The train screeched to a halt and the conductor stuck his head out of a window and frantically yelled something I didn't understand, ending with the word *hospital*. I shook my head no and waved them off; I'd broken no bones. Then I stood up, a bit embarrassed (everyone on the train was looking out the windows at me), brushed myself off, grabbed my luggage, and walked the two miles back to the station.

Okay, so maybe it hadn't been the smartest move. When I got to the station, I found my fall had ripped my heavy sweater all the way up my forearm, leaving a long bloody cut. But the cut wasn't deep, and the Alps were great. So there!

frezzia prodero, originally from Colombia, South America, is a brave Latina who ignores silly old values that say women shouldn't travel alone. She is raising her fantastic, much adored daughter to be just as adventurous.

∞

Hands On, Hands Off
bobbi ausubel

Bobbi's note: *I have two stories, one from girlhood and one from adulthood. You can't miss the common theme: I'm a woman who takes matters into her own hands.*

Growing up female in the 1950s in New York City meant enduring packed subway cars and men who'd bump against you or press their bodies into you. A stranger's hand would find its way here or there, often places you didn't want it. This happened every day on the way to junior high and back. Not only was I young and wavering in confidence, but I was unsure about the groping: *Is this from the normal jostling of the train or are they purposefully doing what I think they are doing?*

One day, though not on the train, I knew for sure. I was sitting in a movie theater with my friend Iris when a man sat down next to me. I knew something was strange because there were lots of empty seats everywhere, but he chose to sit right next to me. Soon after, I felt something crawling around by my behind. It was his hand.

I was confused, and my mind went kind of numb, like it usually did on the subway. Then, an unfamiliar and wild surge of energy built up inside of me and flew out. I grabbed his hand, lifted it way up in the air and screamed at him so loud everyone in the theater could hear: "Does this hand belong to you?"

He got up and walked away.

Iris laughed, shook my hand, and said some 1950s equivalent of "You go, girl!"

Twenty years later, in the early 1970s, I was the director of a small theater on the East Coast. During intermission, I'd stand around in the lobby because I enjoyed listening to people's conversations about the play in progress. One night, a distraught young woman came over to me.

"Somebody took my wallet out of my coat!" She pointed to a man in a long tan overcoat at the other end of the lobby and said, "*That* man was sitting behind me."

Dressed in elegant garb, the guy looked as if he didn't belong in the predominantly hippie crowd my theater drew, so without hesitating, I marched over to him.

"Did you take something from the woman sitting in front of you?" I asked.

Only for an instant did I consider I might be endangering myself by confronting him. At that exact moment I imagined myself Wonder Woman, my childhood heroine. That promptly squashed any rising fears.

"No," the well-mannered man answered, raising his eyebrows as if taken aback.

I didn't buy it.

I pulled his unbuttoned overcoat open wide enough to reach in, fished my hand into the inside pocket, and grabbed the purse it easily landed on. I pulled the red leather pouch out, held it high, and called across the crowded theater lobby to the young woman, "Is this your wallet?"

I was shocked by my own actions, but that soon turned to feelings of triumph, because the surprised woman at the far end of the lobby heard me and nodded yes.

Thinking myself generous, I turned to the man, pointed to the exit, and said, "You can leave now." We didn't believe in calling the police in those days.

bobbi ausubel, a beautifully aging crone playwright and drama teacher, actively misses hippies, because, in truth, nowadays there are hardly any left.

∞

Amen for Sneaky Women
cecelia wambach

The Pope was coming!

Everyone was saying how wonderful this was because he had never come to the United States before and we all knew him to be special—he was a social change activist in Poland, after all. It was 1983. I was teaching at a Catholic women's college in New York City, and like some kid might do with a rock star, I took off three days from work to follow the Pope around as he appeared at various locations.

For the appearance at Yankee Stadium, a colleague gave me two free tickets. I gave one to my friend Bea. We were so excited. But when we arrived, we weren't happy at all; our seats were very, very far back. We were able to see, but not much. Home plate looked like a speck. The stage looked like a dollhouse. Bea and I took off, determined to get closer.

At each new level down we simply pointed south and told the ushers we had seats "down there," and in each case they let us through without actually looking at our tickets. Before this I had had no idea how easy lying could be!

As we proceeded down, we suddenly made it to a layer of cops. It was the honor guard for the Pope, made up of New York's finest, and they all seemed to be Irish Catholic men. Now, you have to imagine the scene here. There were thousands of policemen in the stadium. I mean, the rest of New York was being totally ignored. These blue-uniformed officers paraded around the inside perimeter of the whole stadium, three deep. Just as we made it down to this cop level, the police right in front of us started to line up and march forward. Bea and I joined their line and marched forward with them toward the stage. No one tried to stop us.

Bea grabbed my arm and said, "God is taking care of us. We are invisible."

"What?" I said in disbelief. I didn't know if it was true or not, but it certainly seemed no one was noticing us—two plainclothed women, one Black and one white, in a line of big, burly Irishmen in blue. As I marched, I experienced a fit of laughter, mostly out of fear. *Would they catch us? Arrest us? Shoot us?* I started to pray.

We kept up with the police line and soon we made it onto the field where the symphony was playing and where all the important people sat, such as the cardinals and the rest of the Church hierarchy. When the cops sat down, we did, too. We ended up in a row with about a hundred elite police right in front of the Pope. I mean, *I got to shake his hand!* That night I called my mom to tell her about it and she said she already knew, she'd seen me on TV—live. The next day I saw I was in all the main photos of the event: one hundred policemen, Bea and me, and the Pope.

cecelia maria wambach was a nun for ten years. Now she is a lesbian who never lies. At the start of the third millennium she still loves the Pope.

∞

Fat Grrlz Kick Ass
beth mistretta

You might remember me. I was the girl in your gym class that everyone described as "chubby." I always came in last, heaving and beet-red, when we ran the mile. I hardly ever hit the ball. I wore a shirt two sizes too big in an attempt to hide my body and my shorts, which rode up my inner thighs as I walked. Maybe you acknowledged this by calling me "Heifer," "Bertha," or "Trailer." Until I was sixteen, that was all I encountered in gym class.

Then in 1994, on the first day of my junior year in high school, Ms. L. walked through the door. Ms. L. was the new gym teacher. She was young, fit, and sported a shortish brown haircut that gave her a tomboyish look. She was a skilled camper and could survive in the wilderness for weeks. She preached teamwork, effort, and enthusiasm until we took these as gospel. Most important, she instilled confidence in all of us.

By midsemester, our class was practicing rappelling off our gymnasium balcony. Ms. L. had taught us to handle her high-tech equipment like experts. While we were in action, she paced around the balcony checking our technique and shouting directions as if we were on a real mountain. Once we got the hang of it, we found rappelling to be relatively easy.

Then she taught us how to ascend.

This was the setup: The climbing rope was secured to the balcony. Both the ascender and the belayer wore harnesses that attached them to each other. The climber used a combination of larger ropes and smaller looped ones, as well as metal clamps. Throw on your helmet, stick your foot into the first loop, grab the clamps and climb. Sounds easy, right? Well, when the first boy in our class tried ascending, he sure made it look that way.

In two minutes this boy had climbed twenty feet with barely a drop of sweat on his brow. But when he climbed over the balcony, he exclaimed, "That kicked my ass. That was no joke, man." His words threw all of our confidence out the window. This guy was one of the best in the class, and even he struggled. Despite this, Ms. L. still asked the dreaded question: "Who's next?" We all stared off in different directions and stood in awkward silence, as if she wouldn't notice us if we didn't look at her.

I would be lying if I told you this boy's words brought back all of my lifelong gym-class horrors. Instead, all I could think of was that I was a star in the class, too. I was one of the best rappellers, I had gotten an A on the canoeing skills test, and I had mastered a compass.

My hand darted up and I shouted, "I'll go!"

Some people appeared relieved, though all my girlfriends threw me questioning looks. I avoided eye contact with everyone and created an aura of purpose around me. I was too busy to think twice. I rushed to put on my harness, adjust my ponytail, strap on my helmet, and swagger downstairs. Once at the bottom of the rope, I attached my harness, checked the setup with the belayer on the balcony, got my feet into the ropes, and grabbed my clamps.

"Belayer ready?" I shouted.

"Belayer ready," the student yelled down.

"Ascending," I called out. Before he could even reply, I was off and gone.

Off and gone, that is, until about seven feet into my climb, when I became exhausted—deeply exhausted—and came to a dead stop.

I sat dangling from the rope with my harness painfully digging into my butt and inner thighs. I stretched to pull up the looped ropes so that I could step into them and keep going. Unfortunately, I pulled them too high and could not move them down. Suddenly, the absurdity of climbing up with no ground below to push against struck me. In my tight jeans, my leg battled to defy gravity to get my foot into the damn loop. It felt too difficult. I began to panic. I considered giving up, yet I knew how humiliated I would be if the whole class had to watch the belayer lower me down.

Ms. L. sensed my frustration and began to coach and encourage me. "This is not hard, Beth. I know you can do this. Just get that foot in there and push your body up. Move it!"

I tried, and tried again, and finally I got my foot into the loop. I grabbed the clamps with my hands and felt my quads, hamstrings, and biceps strain as I pulled myself up. I looked above at the balcony: about halfway to go.

Honestly, the rest of the climb was not much easier. I summoned upper-body strength I never knew I had. I mean, you're talking about someone who couldn't even do a single pull-up. Then, after one more excruciating rest on my pinching harness, my face met the floor of the balcony. I was almost there. With a surge of optimism (or was it adrenaline?), suddenly my work became effortless. Within seconds I was climbing over the balcony bars while Ms. L. commanded to the belayer, "Pull her in, pull her in. Don't let her go yet!"

When I was standing on the balcony, both feet on solid ground, I took off my helmet and my head looked as if I had showered. I was heaving, my face was bright red, and sweat ran down my neck. By this time, everyone was clapping. I was the first girl at East High School to ascend. I tried to look humble, but it wasn't working. I now knew I could run with the best of them, and I figured, why not smile about it?

Yeah, sure, **beth mistretta** (emistre@aol.com) did graduate with a journalism degree from a good Chicago university, and did get a job in her field as Community News Coordinator for a daily newspaper. But way more important, she is also a fitness instructor at an all-women's health club, where she's been teaching since shortly after taking Ms. L.'s class.

∞

Paying for It
monique bowden

We'd been warned it was too dangerous to go out into the dark streets of Detroit, but I was hungry and so was Alice. We left the safety of our conference site at Cobal Hall and headed for a diner we'd spotted earlier.

When we arrived at the little corner eating establishment, we were frozen, and decided it would be in our best interest to take a cab back to the convention center when we finished dinner. As we took our booth, we were happy to see a taxi pull into the cabstand and the driver come inside for his own supper. I asked him if we could be his first fare after his meal. He agreed. Knowing that we wouldn't freeze on the walk back to the convention center, Alice and I sipped hot tea and settled into the warm comfort of the diner. Within minutes our food was placed in front of us.

I had barely taken a bite of my hamburger when the front doors of the restaurant flew open. In stepped a hip-swinging parade of four meticulously groomed women draped in full-length white mink coats. Two showed off their majestic breasts in white dresses with necklines that plunged to the waist; two wore red dresses with spaghetti straps molded over their petite bodies. All had on six-inch stiletto heels, which they walked in effortlessly.

This impressive ensemble was watched over by a tall, slender man wrapped in a white mink coat and white mink hat. His suit was red, and the wind blew his coat open just enough to reveal a shiny lining that perfectly matched the crimson color of the ladies' dresses.

Alice whispered, "Those are real hookers!"

"And you know what that makes *him*," I said, and we started to giggle.

Our laughter snagged the attention of the man in mink. He moonwalked backward, came to a dead halt in front of our table, snatched off his Blues Brothers sunglasses, threw his hands in the air and sang, "Ladies!" He pulled out a chair and sat down at our table.

Alice gathered her belongings and slid one arm into her coat. I was about to follow her lead when I noticed the women who had come in with him were seated at a nearby table, snickering at our fright. My internal defense mechanism clicked. I have never been one to be intimidated, and I wasn't about to start now. I touched Alice's arm to reassure her, then addressed the gentleman: "I didn't hear anyone ask you to sit down."

"I couldn't let you ladies pass up on the opportunity to have a little chit-chat with a man such as myself."

What made him think that either of us wanted to talk to him, I'll never know. But I knew from his boldness that he wasn't going to leave just because he was asked. I decided to talk to him in a way I thought he would understand.

"In order to have a chit-chat without an invitation, you'll need to lay fifty dollars on the table."

In my peripheral vision I saw Alice's mouth drop. I kept my main focus on the man, who also seemed a bit surprised, though he quickly recovered.

I repeated myself in a sterner tone. "If you are going to sit here, you'll have to lay fifty dollars on the table. Otherwise, move on."

"You got nerve," he said, unmoved.

"Yes," I said. I pointed to his female companions, "Look, you don't let them sit and chitchat for free. I'm not going to give you my time for nothin', either. Now pay or go."

I expected him to leave, to maybe laugh and go away. Instead, he reached into his pocket, pulled out a roll of money, peeled off a fifty-dollar bill and cast it on the table. "I respect a *business-woman*," he said, as he casually leaned back in his chair.

He had called my bluff.

I picked up the money. Fearful of where my gamble might take me, I said, "That will buy you fifteen minutes of conversation, and it doesn't have to be polite."

The man began waving his arms like a choir director, while he rhymed and sang words as though he had memorized lines from some horrible off-Broadway play. As I ate, I watched his fanfare of body jerks and head bobs, with his fingers flaring and snapping. Though he had an impressive command of the English language, I found him irritating, annoying, despicable. I became insulted when he told me in singsong, "If-you-can'tcomprehend-what-I-recommend, I'll-just-back-up-and-come-again."

I gladly interrupted him: "Your fifteen minutes are up. Either put another fifty on the table or leave."

"Baby, you ain't said nothing but a word." With arrogance he reached for his money roll a second time and threw another fifty on the table. I put the money away and he continued his performance as if the interruption had never occurred.

After a few more minutes I saw the cabdriver head for the counter with cash in hand. I got Alice's attention and nodded toward the checkout and our ride. I put on my coat and picked up the check.

"Where you think you're going? I still got time on the clock."

I checked my watch. He still had six minutes left from his second fifty dollars. I smiled and said, "That just mean you won't have to lay out the money to pay for our dinners."

I strolled off to pay the check, relieved to be out of his presence. And I was quite pleased with myself when I heard him say, "Aw man, she got my money. She played me, y'all. She played the player."

monique bowden, originally from Guyana, loves to travel. She has visited sixteen countries—seventeen, if you count the Republic of Detroit. She resides in the warm south of Tallahassee, Florida, and used her hard-earned money to pamper herself with a day at the salon.

Selling the Berlin Wall
rivka solomon

When the Berlin Wall "fell" in November 1989, there was nothing else on TV. I sat stunned, watching hordes of East and West Berliners streaming through gates finally opened to them after decades of separation. Revelers climbed on top of the wall itself, popping champagne corks and toasting what appeared to be the end of the Cold War. For three solid days the world was glued to CNN as German citizens furiously hammered at the graffiti-covered west side of the wall. Picks, axes, and jackhammers were meeting its miles and miles of concrete. Apparently these folks thought they could slowly chip the wall out of existence. And they were right.

This was history happening—a once-in-a-lifetime occurrence. So what was a recent political science graduate, an international relations buff, to do? Well, duh. Go.

Jobless and flat broke, I borrowed airfare from my mom and promised to have it back in a week. One week. Now I wasn't being totally irresponsible; I had a plan. It wasn't exactly one of those thought-through kind of plans; in fact, I suppose it was more closely related to an impulse. Two days before I hopped on the plane, I had come across a small paragraph in one of the many newspapers jam-packed with banner headlines, huge photos, and full-page accounts of the wall's fall. A mere two lines, it said some entrepreneurial East Berlin kids were making a killing selling tourists bits of wall they'd chipped off. I packed my bags.

When my backpack slid down the Berlin airport baggage ramp and onto the carousel for passengers to collect, I could hear the pick and hammer I'd stowed away clank against each other. And I wasn't alone. Two other backpacks from my flight clanked the same way when they landed. One belonged to a fellow young American who confessed he was there to collect wall and make a buck. The second belonged to a big Irishman, also our age, who wanted to see history as it happened, and bring home a souvenir. Ideologically, I was somewhere in between the two. The three of us instantly bonded.

Although our flight had landed late at night, we three went straight to the wall to scout out the work ahead of us. Within minutes of arriving at the daunting structure (it was much more imposing in person than on TV), and within seconds of putting pick to concrete, we realized this was just about the hardest iron-rod-reinforced concrete any of us had ever seen—let alone tried to dismantle.

From then on, I spent nearly every waking moment at the wall. Either I was holding extraordinary conversations about glasnost, perestroika, and the end of the Cold War with any of the thousands of Berliners and tourists flocking around, or I was hammering. Every few feet along the wall's perimeter, someone was taking a crack at it. In a few rare places the wall had been slowly, methodically, smashed through. There we could squeeze in between the bent iron rods and into East Berlin's barren no-man's-land, where only a week earlier someone could have been shot for standing.

By night, my two pals and I met up again only to collapse on incredibly uncomfortable cots in the cheapest and therefore most rundown hotel we could find. Rundown, yes, but they did provide strong pillowcases. Three days after I arrived, I left Berlin with a hotel pillowcase full of concrete, weighing in on the airport scale at ninety pounds. I also left the city with two rolls of film: proof of the authenticity of my goods. ("Pardon me, sir, would you mind taking a picture of me with my camera as I hammer at the wall. It's for my mother.")

Once back home, rushing, I put each chip of wall in its own plastic sandwich bag. The coveted pieces were the ones with graffiti paint on them. I got lots. Also in each bag, I slipped a photocopy of a pathetically short description of the Cold War and its apparent demise (all those years as a Poli Sci major had finally paid off). I headed to New York, dragging my boyfriend with me. We drove the five hours to the city, pulled off the highway, and illegally parked in a loading zone five feet from Macy's front door. I set up shop. My boyfriend stayed in the car and watched my back as I unfolded my tiny portable table. It was rush hour, December 22. Oy, were those Christians in a frenzy, eager to buy the hottest gift that year (was it Cabbage Patch dolls?), or anything at all, since there were only (ready to panic?) *two shopping days left before Christmas.*

I unfolded the cardboard display I'd made. It included my airline tickets and the photos of me at the wall, pick in hand. Suddenly I was surrounded. Everyone wanted a piece of me, or at least the wall.

"How much? How much?" they shouted at once.

"Look, she was really there," others cried, pointing to my display.

"Great stocking stuffers!" I heard someone say.

My prices were reasonable: $5 to $25, depending on the size. It was a tad chaotic, but in ten minutes I made over $350—the cost of my airline ticket. I was elated, and I still had eighty-six pounds of wall left. From the car, my boyfriend beeped and pointed behind him. I saw a truck on his butt and knew he had to go. I nodded, sure he would zip 'round the block and be back in a flash.

Then a man asked me how much for a certain piece. "Ten," I told him without looking up. And why should I? I was busy taking money from some lady buying three bags.

"Wow. They're real, too," the man continued. "I see that from the plane ticket. That's great. I'll take one. Say, do you have a permit to sell on the street?"

"Huh? Uh, no," I said, glancing up for the first time. He appeared to be a harmless if disheveled working guy.

"Oh, well then . . . " and with that, he flashed a police badge, swept my entire display, pieces of wall, and folding table into a huge garbage bag, handcuffed me, and whistled for a blue van to pick me up—all in about two seconds flat. I was inside that van with five other offenders before you could say *'Tis the season to be jolly*.

I had to work to keep from crying. "When my boyfriend comes back," I sniffled out the window to the vendor who'd been legally hawking Jesus bookmarks right next to me, "tell him I was arrested."

He offered me a sympathetic look and said, "You need a permit."

No kidding.

I sat with my handcuffed wrists behind my back for the next hour as we picked up a half dozen other permitless vendors and their wares. Sunglasses, teddy bears, pocketbooks, watches—all now in police-sealed garbage bags lying at our feet. Evidence. We were brought to a huge gymlike room, lined up with others, and fingerprinted. I became a bit of a celebrity. They'd never confiscated the Berlin Wall before. "It's real! I saw the photos," the excited arresting officer told his colleagues.

I was separated from the other vendors and brought to my own cage; after all, I was the only woman in the bunch. Before I could sit on the floor to ponder what to do next (like I had a choice), a plainclothed cop advanced toward me, screaming, "Don't I know you? Aren't you the punk bitch who ran away last week when I tried to arrest you?"

"No," I squeaked, backing up, though my cage would only let me go so far.

Satisfied he'd sufficiently shaken me up (and he had), the pit-bull cop withdrew and I was left alone in my six-by-six.

Then, a few hours later, at about 10:00 P.M., just as suddenly as I had been taken in, I heard "Get outta here." In what appeared to be a whimsical decision, one of my captors swatted the air with his backhand, indicating he had bestowed freedom upon me. Dazed, I nodded, walked out the door and onto the dark street. I had no idea where I was, but at least I wasn't in jail anymore.

Amazingly, my boyfriend had found me and was waiting outside in my car. We hugged, cried about how scary it had all been, and then went to my grandmother's apartment to visit, pretending we had *just* rolled off the highway and into New York City. (She didn't even know I'd gone to Berlin.)

Three weeks later, a court-appointed lawyer I met thirty seconds before my hearing pleaded with the judge to let me off. The judge rolled his eyes, "Pieces of the Berlin Wall. Right, sure. Whadda scam."

"They're real," I barked back, New York–style.

My lawyer told me to sit down and shut up. I did, and impressively he got the case dismissed—as long as I didn't get rear-rested in the upcoming year. That seemed doable.

A month later, I drove the five hours back to New York, this time to visit the city's huge—football-field-huge—Confiscated Goods Warehouse. I was on a mission to collect my wall, and quite worried it might have gotten lost or stolen during the ordeal. History-in-the-making is not easily replaced. When I opened the sealed evidence bag, I was elated; it all appeared to be there, though I bet the arresting officer had taken a handful. Unlike the judge, he had believed me.

rivka solomon still has eighty-six pounds of Berlin Wall sitting in a dusty box in her mother's basement.

∽

Educating Bill Clinton
bonnie morris

I am a professor at George Washington University in Washington, D.C., and an avid supporter of our women's basketball team. In 1995, when I attended the homecoming doubleheader (men's and women's games back-to-back), I was startled to be sent through a metal detector. What's up with this? I asked. Had someone threatened our teams? No, a colleague told me, President Clinton was visiting. And he had brought his daughter, Chelsea, to our event. After all, the White House was only down the road.

First the men played, and won. During intermission the President congratulated them. On his way out, he made himself accessible to the crowd and shook hands with nearly everyone. I was amazed at how easy it was to greet him. I pushed my way through the stands to shake the President's hand.

"Hi, Mr. President," I said. "I teach women's history here at GWU. I think it would be real meaningful, and an important statement to your daughter, if you'd stay and watch the women's game." Determination smoothed my bravery along, so I pointedly added, "Don't leave now that the men's team has won. Show your support of Title IX and women athletes."

"Well, I'd like to stay," Bill Clinton told me. "But I have a meeting at two o'clock."

"Fine," I replied, feeling sure of my convictions as well as my temporal calculations. "You can still watch the first twenty minutes of the women's game." To my delight, the President went back to his seat and cheered the women on.

I'd just given a direct order to the president of the United States, and he took it.

Later, he became the first president ever to telephone his congratulations to the winning *women's* team of the NCAA basketball championships. I'd like to think I had a little something to do with that.

bonnie morris, a.k.a. Dr. Bon, is a Women's Studies professor, lesbian activist, and nice Jewish girl. The three combined, by definition, means she's got the chutzpah to order *anyone* around.

∞

Saving Mommy, or The Night I Lost My Childhood
d. h. wu

"Honey, wake up. Wake up, baby, okay?"

"Mommy? What's wrong? What happened?"

"Wake up, honey. Put your kimono, we go. I get your brother. Hurry up."

"What? Where are we going?"

"Be a good girl and listen Mommy, okay? Help Mommy, please, baby. Help Mommy."

She sounded more frantic, more desperate than I'd ever heard her. *They must have fought again,* I thought. Now, in the middle of the night, we would "go" one more time. Instead of the usual harried grabbing of extra changes of clothes, this time she simply dressed my younger brother in his robe and slippers and asked me to do the same. I complied. There would be no reasoning with her until we got out of the house and away. I figured we were going to a phone booth, as usual, where we'd wait for a cab or friend to pick us up, and where I'd be able to reason with her.

We walked into the street. The sky was clear and full of stars, the night silent and chilled—rare for summer in Taiwan. Everything and everyone in the world seemed forever gone.

Mommy walked hurriedly with my brother in her arms, her high heels failing her in her struggle to move faster. She moaned. It was that noise that always scared me, the one that came from the darkest, most unknowable part of the soul. She cried and muttered endlessly—half in Chinese, half in broken English—about how much she hated him, about how she couldn't take it, about how she wouldn't stand it . . . about how she didn't want to live any more. As she rushed past the phone booth, I jogged beside her, trying to keep my little six-year-old legs in pace with hers. My mind was in a fevered state: *Where are we going? What should I do? What should I say?*

We approached the train tracks and I suddenly understood. She was prone to extremes. I knew the years of getting banged against walls, cut with knives, threatened with guns, kicked, punched, stepped on; years of broken bones, torn ligaments, and unborn children pummeled into miscarriage had led her to the desperation and anger I was now seeing. It was the blood, the bruises, the fear and misery, day after day, year after year, that finally brought us to those tracks.

As her tirade subsided, her voice began to grow clear. Her

despair gave way to an intent to persuade, and she became eerily convincing to me as she spoke. "Okay, baby, that's it. Mommy no take his crap no more. That's right, we come back in the next life and try again. We do better, okay? We leave him for good. I can't take any more, baby. Mommy get you and you brother better father *next time,* okay baby?"

Next time: Usually, for Buddhists like Mom, that means the next life; on this night, for her, it also meant freedom.

Everything stopped, time stood still. The first thought that finally formed in my mind was *I'm only six. I'm not ready to die.* Though the promise of the three of us leaving him forever and coming back to a new father, a good one, was better than I could imagine. But no, I just wasn't ready, not yet.

As I listened to her frenzied reasonings, I became conscious that the ground was rumbling under us, that the once faint clack-clacking in the distance was growing urgent: The train was coming. I flew into a panic.

"Mommy, wait! No, no, it's okay. We don't have to die. We can just leave him. We'll do it right now. We don't have to die!" I looked up at her: "Mommy, *I don't want to die.*"

She nodded slowly, understanding, but only half persuaded. She handed my brother to me, "Okay, Mommy go alone."

I started again, "Mommy, *no!* It's okay, it's okay. You don't have to die. Just leave him! You don't want to die, I know you don't. He'll win if you die. Mommy, *don't leave us with him by ourselves!*"

I pleaded, with my brother clinging around my neck while I struggled to keep him from slipping off me. Tears and mucous streamed out of my eyes and nose. I tugged at her wrist to pull her away from the tracks she was inching toward.

"Mommy, don't leave me, please! It'll be okay. Please, please, Mommy. I love you. *I'll take care of you! I promise! I promise!"*

With that promise, she finally broke.

She moved away from the rail and lay flat on the ground, wailing. Her agony echoed out through the fields, toward the houses nearby, yet no one came to help. I stood there relieved, panting, watching her sob in defeat. The train sped past, so close we could almost reach out to touch it.

That was the first time I saved my mother's life.

We understood from that moment on we'd indefinitely bound ourselves to the evil we'd wanted so desperately to escape. She was trapped, doomed to suffer the beatings over and over for the sake of her children. And it was my job, ever after, to protect her—even at the cost of an innocent childhood. We knew we only had each other. There was no one else to help us.

Sometimes I could block a punch or throw a few, talk down a gun or even brandish one. Sometimes I put a stop to it; but more often than not, he would beat her until she was nothing but a bloodied, terrified mess, crying in a corner. Yet I never gave up my attempts to save her.

She finally divorced him before I reached my teen years, thereby exonerating us both from our promise to each other. Now that he's dead, we both know to simply enjoy the freedom and quiet that was so elusive to us in those earlier days. If you listen closely, though, you can hear our secret history in the way I still call her my "Mommy" and she still calls me her "Baby."

d. h. wu (hapagrrl1@yahoo.com) dedicates this to every girl and woman who has ever been rescued, been the rescuer herself, or who may need rescuing right now. Today no one needs to live through this abuse. Today there are people who can help.

For confidential 24-hour help, contact:
National Domestic Violence Hotline
P.O. Box 161810
Austin, TX 78716
Phone: (800) 799-SAFE (7233)
TDD: (800) 787-3224
Website: www.ndvh.org

For additional twenty-four-hour assistance in locating local services and shelters for battered women and men, call 411.

∞

Nothing from Nobody
tara betts

Fridays were our days. When she was still tending bar at the tavern she and Grandpa owned, my grandmother would take me home with her after closing. My daddy worked in the tavern, too, and I lived and slept with my parents in the apartment above. But not on weekends. That was when we'd sit in Grandma's orange kitchen shucking corn, shelling peas, and telling stories. I looked forward to midnight on Fridays when the jukebox stopped and I'd wait on the steps with an old, gray bowling bag packed for a sleepover. Together, Grandma and I would hop into her burgundy Buick Regal to go to her home, little more than five minutes away.

One night a stranger interrupted this memorable routine before we even got to the house. This stranger had a siren and a badge.

When most people see me, especially now that I'm older, they say I look just like my grandmother. I think so, too. Some people have a hard time recognizing it though, probably because they expect us to have the same skin color and hair texture. Instead, I have the complexion and hair of my white mother. My grandmother thinks that's why the police officer pulled her over, because maybe he thought she'd kidnapped this five-year-old white child.

This is where she begins her version of the story, which she says reflects the Tara I grew up to be: "So, they pulled me over, and the one officer starts talking to me, and he shines the flashlight on my face, and he's asking me questions—and then he starts asking about Tara."

What my grandmother doesn't say when she's telling this story is what she must have been feeling as that flashlight blinded her. Was it humiliation at being questioned so suspiciously for simply being Black? Maybe she felt fear, because who knows what crimes white cops committed against Black women in the 1970s, on dark, quiet streets so late at night? Whatever she was feeling, I sensed it.

"About this time," Grandma continues, "Tara, who never was one for sitting still, jumps up in the seat and goes"—Grandma makes a sideways-looking face that imitates me about to snap—"'What'chu doin' puttin' that light in my granma's face? You betta get that light out my granma's face! What'chu think you doin'?!'"

"So, I guess he figured I didn't steal you from nobody," she said, the last time I heard her tell the story. She stifles her laughter when she gets to this part, just like she says she did then, when the undoubtedly bewildered and embarrassed officer wished her a good night and walked back to his squad car.

I don't remember this incident, but I'll take Grandma's word that it happened. After all, she *is* right that it reflects the Tara I grew up to be: *I won't take nothing from nobody.*

tara betts (tarabetts@aol.com) creates semantic soups as a creative writing instructor, poetry slam team member, and cohost of a monthly all-women open mike in Chicago. She is currently working on a book of poems about Ida B. Wells. To this day, though no longer having sleepovers at her grandmother's house, Tara won't let anyone step to Grandma, or any woman, the wrong way.

I Swear!
louise civetti

A number of years ago, I was invited to attend a technical meeting at an extremely conservative corporation. When I say it was conservative, I am talking about the fact that the company had been in business for more than a hundred years, and I was the first female to attend one of these meetings.

During the meeting of the "good ol' boys," the air in the room became heated, faces red, collars tight, and the language, well, let's just say, *colorful*. All eyes turned to me. I pretended not to notice.

Once the meeting concluded, my boss pulled me aside and said, "I'm sorry the language got out of hand in there." I told him his apology was accepted, but that next time he'd better watch his f***ing mouth.

louise civetti didn't lose her job for at least a couple of years after that.

∽

You Can Take That Law and . . .
gwyn mcvay

During my college days, I was one of the founding officers of our local chapter of NORML, the National Organization for the Reform of Marijuana Laws. I believed, among other things, that the police should concentrate more on arresting rapists than on chasing basement joint-smokers, and that medical patients ought to have access to this remedy for a variety of ills ranging from cancer and AIDS to severe menstrual cramps (like I had).

We enjoyed a lot of support on campus, but the conservative local population tended to react differently. One day two friends and I were downtown putting up posters and handing out flyers for a NORML benefit concert we were holding at the VFW (those Veterans of Foreign Wars are so hip!). We were doing nothing illegal. Before long, two cops came and plunked themselves down right next to us, not saying anything, just making their presence clearly known. My friends became visibly upset.

"Are they trying to censor us?" said one, nervously picking up and putting down our pile of flyers.

"Can they force us to move on?" another asked, walking around and around in little circles.

"I don't know," I said. More than anything, I felt curious—and ready to be challenged. Instead of waiting to find out their intentions, I took some of our literature, went up to the men in blue, introduced myself, and handed each a flyer.

My friends were astonished; the cops accepted the flyers and in the ensuing conversation turned out to be quite reasonable and agreeable. ("Would you like to come to our benefit concert tonight?" I asked. "Thank you; I'll think about it," one said.)

We talked for a while, then *they* moved on, and we all continued with a pleasant afternoon.

gwyn mcvay was raised to question authority.

CHAPTER 2

After Some Thought: Making Life-changing Choices

Making deliberate decisions

Contemplative

REFLECTIVE

Not all gutsy acts come straight from the gut. Some make pit stops, even linger for a while in our heads. There we study the consequences, weigh the options, and make choices—not on the fly, but after deep thought. This chapter is about premeditated personal decisions. Decisions about THE BIG THINGS: health, family, career, where and how to spend a life.

In these stories, women reassess their paths in the world and subsequently map out alternate routes. They make choices and commitments that lead to radical transformations. Sometimes acting without role models or support, sometimes taking the risk of going against conventional wisdom, the women here think for themselves and let their internal strength guide them.

Listening to their inner, kickboxing Buddha, whose savvy wisdom they know to be true, makes the women in this chapter stronger, especially when, donning gloves and entering the ring, they know the match could be lonely or difficult. Trusting themselves when times are tough shows firmness of character, determination—feistiness!

So while these more pensive deeds may at first appear slower and softer than others in this book, let's be real—they are among some of the bravest a woman can carry out in her lifetime.

Double Whammy
lynda gaines

My first surgery was a piece of cake, and necessary to remove a lump that I knew to my core would not be cancerous. In fact, the lump itself wasn't. If it hadn't been for those other "funny-looking cells" they shipped off to Yale, all would have been well.

Every woman who hears "breast cancer" in her doctor's office is courageous. Keeping fears in check and making decisions under the cloud of "chance of recurrence" is difficult. So is keeping life as normal as possible while seeing a variety of specialists, doing mind- and body-altering drug therapy, enduring daily radiation appointments, and undergoing radical surgery. Even with support, one is very much alone; no two diagnoses, attitudes, and situations are the same. In the end, the individual herself makes the decisions. Brave women do it every day.

Yale found that the "funny-looking cells" were indeed early cancer. So just before Christmas, I had a second surgery to remove this material, which was then sent to my hospital's Tumor Board for review. I tried not to let any of it impact my holiday spirit, but it did. Exhausted and frightened, I cried through office parties, family dinners, and Rudolph reruns. My surgeon tried to reassure me.

"My gut feeling, Lynda, is there won't be more surgery."

That's good, I thought, *because there's* no way *I'll be able to deal with a mastectomy.*

Then I got the call.

The cancerous material was well dispersed throughout my left breast. The Tumor Board said the best bet was to remove the whole thing. I was in shock. The good news was that no additional treatment would be necessary. No mind-numbing, vomit-inducing therapy, no daily radiation appointments. The bad news was that after doing my homework (two second opinions), it looked like, yes, a mastectomy was in my future.

Once I had accepted the inevitable, I felt strongly that I didn't want to have only one breast. To me, it was out of balance, and more shameful.

"I'll feel embarrassed," I said to my husband, "answering the door or running out for a video with only one breast. I'd always want to hide it."

Besides, my mother had raised me to be a nudie. One of my greatest joys was going to parent-child swimming classes at the YMCA and taking a shower afterward with my two-year-old. Stripped of our suits, together we'd play and scrub openly in the shower. I'd been doing it for years with my kids. With only one breast, I feared I'd feel too self-conscious and would give that up.

No, one breast just didn't feel right. *If I have to remove one,* I decided, *then I'll remove both.*

That's what my gut said, but was that the right decision? Was I being misled by my own instincts? I began talking to women who had had mastectomies. I was searching for someone who'd "cut them *both* off," hadn't gotten reconstructive surgery, and hadn't looked back. I wanted to find a no-breasted woman who was happy: someone in whose footsteps I could follow (easier to follow than lead!). But I couldn't find her. The closest I got was hearing about a book that profiled post-mastectomy women. I was told it included one woman who spoke of how free she felt without breasts, how the surgery had given her back that preadolescent "tomboy" time in her life. I couldn't find the book, but it helped knowing this woman was out there somewhere in the world.

Apparently, she was unusual. Most women I talked with were excited about reconstruction. They wanted to convince me how real it looked and felt. I was glad they'd been able to come through a difficult experience feeling whole and positive about the decisions they'd made. However, my inner voice continued to say no—reconstruction did *not* appeal to me. Go through yet another surgery either for implants or to have a piece of my abdominal muscle cut out and stitched to my chest? For what? *Breasts? Who cares?* That's how I felt.

I talked to everyone in my life. They all agreed to support me in whatever I did, but I still felt alone in making my choice. A few weeks before my surgery, I had dinner with my four closest women friends. We started joking about the *advantages* of having no breasts. Our Top Ten list helped me face my surgery with courage and, just as important, humor.

My surgeon was surprised by my choice for a double mastectomy. However, since he knew I could always opt for reconstruction later, he didn't try to talk me out of it. I felt in my heart I would be fine without breasts. Even though I could find no role model I could talk to, no one who had gone before me, I did it anyway.

The surgery went well; I healed quickly. And you know what? I haven't looked back. I feel free! No more bras! In some ways, I even feel sexier than I did before. At home I still walk around naked before my husband and children without shame, and I don't hide myself in a changing booth at the Y. No, it hasn't been easy. I have had to work on rebuilding my body image. I joined a gym and started lifting weights again. Though I sometimes contemplate donning a prosthesis C-cup for a special occasion, so far I am living flat-chested with absolutely no regrets about my decision.

When I talk to women now facing a mastectomy, I know the chances are slim they will follow in my footsteps. I talk about how free I feel, and they listen politely. Then they tell me they will reconstruct. I keep telling my story, however, hoping that someday, when another woman makes the choice I did, she will know she isn't alone.

The Top Ten Advantages to Having Both Breasts Removed

10. Quick way to lose a few pounds.

9. If bad things happen in threes, this counts for two.

8. Wardrobe overhaul required.

7. One less excuse for not running a marathon.

6. Guaranteed to knock six strokes off your golf game.

5. No more mammograms.

4. Makes cross-dressing a whole lot easier.

3. Every morning you get to decide if you want to be an A, B, C, D—or no cup at all!

2. "Hey, baby, want to see my mastectomy scars?" makes a great pickup line.

1. You will never be mistaken for a waitress at Hooters.

lynda gaines, manager of telesales for a small software company in Jamestown, Rhode Island, sent this submission in on a dare from her mother (the one who raised her to be a nudie, remember?). Lynda's mama, who is also a breast-cancer survivor, feels her daughter is bold and courageous for making her choice. She thought her role-model daughter should share the experience so other women could explore all their options, too.

∞

Divine Perfection
anitra winder

I was born twenty-six years ago to my mother, my closest stranger. Sonya was only eighteen, a rambling teenager in the projects of Baltimore. She conceived me with one of the popular neighborhood Black studs. But Sonya had a lot of traffic coming her way, so it's anybody's guess who daddy is. With my creation came years of poverty, regret, and upheaval. We lived a nomadic existence, never laying our heads anywhere for long.

My unstable childhood walked hand in hand with an unstable education. During bouts of depression over a lost love, Sonya would be far too miserable to see me off to school. I stayed at home and consoled her with my homemade macaroni valentines, sprinkled with glitter and love. To my disappointment, I'd later find them in the trash. I was too young to understand; my love wasn't enough. My love was too small. It was only five years old.

Sonya was lukewarm and always longing. She swore all would be right with the world if she could just have a man at night. Not some nights, every night. I saw many come and go, because whereas Sonya may have equated happiness with a man, she never kept one for long. "Meet Uncle Conrad," "Meet Uncle Larry," she'd say, and I'd think to myself, *You only have one brother, where the rest come from?* I was overwhelmed with lost uncles who found their way home by way of her bed.

The years went by, I grew older, and my mother's past became a guide to my future. When I was seventeen, she was newly married. Her last words to me cut to the bone: "I finally have a life," she said, "and now you need to find your own." I wasn't to return because she was finished raising me. It was that simple. I slept at the Greyhound station that night, a discarded product of discord. It didn't take long before I realized sex was an ever-present trade for a warm bed and a hot plate.

I am ashamed of the company I've kept. Other women's husbands, boyfriends, fathers, sons. I offer no excuses, just the truth about the depths I traveled for the sake of self-preservation. Young and ignorant, I fell unnoticed into the shadows of our society. While others my age were celebrating their graduation from the university of *this* and getting their degree in *that,* I gave up my ass in a dirty hotel in Hollywood.

Lying on my back, I'd look right through whoever was on me. Breath stinking of gin or beer, their sweaty bodies pushed and shoved inside me. Every day, lists of phone numbers of Johns and Mikes who'd pay a buck or two to see a friend and me "Do what dykes do." Me on top, her on the bottom. *It doesn't matter,* I told myself, *'cause it'll all be over when the money hits the bed and he closes the door.*

I tried to suppress my cowardly inclinations. Suicide could never be a successful escape, yet it whispered to me once or twice—I have the ugly scars from our past dances together. I'd fantasize about being found dead, beautifully draped across my bed. At my funeral, I'd hover above, watching the monsoon of tears. *How lovely,* I'd think, *the world really did care.*

One night I stood at the mirror, patching my face together after a trick nearly split my head apart with a baseball bat. I craved rebirth. Evolution. I was growing sick of the husbands, sick of the boyfriends. Sick of spreading my legs.

Finally, barely twenty-one, I abandoned my old life in hopes of living a new one.

In the beginning, I stood on the back of our prized public assistance programs to help me gain my sea legs. It was not easy returning to society when for so long I'd looked up at it from the gutter. Help was fleeting, empathy was rare. People were dismissive and disapproving. They rarely looked me in the eyes, as if they'd catch my misfortune. Even my social worker wasn't supportive. She glared at me over her Coke-bottle glasses with the warmth of a cobra. *How can she help me,* I wondered, *when she doesn't believe in me?*

I began my venture into the mainstream timidly. First I bought an old car. Then I drove twenty miles to a temp office, wearing a $10 suit, scuffed-up sneakers, and a glow of anticipation. Intimidated but hopeful, I listened to my job description. I bit the inside of my jaw raw wondering if they knew what I was.

I soon sat on an assembly line. Eight hours a day, plus overtime, for $4.25 an hour. It was a hundred degrees in that warehouse where I shoved "talk boxes" up stuffed-bunny butts. I sweated and stuffed for months, and with my earnings moved into a clean, furnished single. For the first time I worked without the weight of shame and came home to a quiet place that was mine. It was dreadfully lonely, but I took comfort in the fact that the bed I slept in was used for just that and nothing more. Even so, I rarely felt the calm cover of sleep. In my dreams I'd see them: men's haggard and twisted faces hissing my name. They bound me, pushing me to my knees. I remembered, though I wished I wouldn't.

Even now, in the stillness of my room, I often wake a few hours before dawn. I greet the morning perched on the back stairs, inhaling the sweetness of my Newports. I watch the crossover of daybreak. Down the way I sometimes see a couple of "boulevard girls" seeking refuge from the rising sun. *God, they look younger than I was. Poor lost little girls.*

No, all is not yet right in the world.

But at the same time, I think about this new world of mine. I am amazed at the changes time can bring. I now have a new job, paying a good wage. *What else awaits me?* It's a joy to ponder my opportunities.

One recent morning, gazing into the sun, I realized for the first time my divine perfection. The creator of all things thought I was special enough to be blessed with the gift of life. I cried. And right then and there I let go of the deprived and painful way I was raised and how that helped shape me into who I came to be. I let go of the hatred. I decided to live. Whore. Virgin. Nigga bitch. Beloved. I am all. For all these things have made a complete me, in sorrow and now in peace.

anitra winder is a fat Black lesbian who is now HaPpY with life. She feels that all women's stories should be heard: "This is only one of many that depict the great accomplishments of everyday women—women like you! We are all queens."

∞

Cinderella, Ph.D.

iris stammberger

It was almost midnight, and the Pacific Ocean's warm breeze waltzed through the enormous panoramic windows of the villa. I could hear the waves and smell the salty mist. They were perfect complements to the exquisite European and South American delicacies Alain, our host, had set out. He wanted to please me, the consultant responsible for the final destiny of the project. I was catered to like Cinderella at the ball.

"*¡Fantástico!*"

"*¡Qué bueno!*"

Guests talked in superlatives about the project, and they appreciated my role in shaping it. It was a wonderful full-moon night and I felt it like a reward. After years of hard work, despite the criticism from colleagues that "two women could not succeed in this market," my business partner and I had created the first women-owned engineering consulting firm in Venezuela. Without compromising our integrity, we had won important contracts in our country and were establishing a solid presence in others.

Even competitors who had initially laughed at us were finally convinced we were there to stay. They stopped offering me enticing executive positions; now they wanted to buy our firm. With market recognition came more money, resources, and contracts. I had climbed the ladder and made it to the top. My presence in Alain's country and my stewardship of the project was proof.

But despite this success, something was deeply wrong.

At the magnificent villa, I appeared at ease sitting among the elite representatives of the government agency that would borrow and administer the money, the prestigious officials of the Euro-American consortium that would build the project, and a local politician who teared up as he joyfully declared, "This electrical and agro-industrial facility will *forever* change our region."

The next morning I would fly to Washington to report to the international development agency that had hired me. It had been my job to ensure that the project followed environmental standards and that the indigenous people affected by the development would be adequately considered. After much hard work, I was proud of what I had achieved. Yet beneath the polite conversation I wondered, *Why, instead of the pleasure of accomplishment, do I feel immense sadness?*

I searched for clarity in the faces around me. First, our host, a handsome South American millionaire who believed he was doing his nation a favor by administering the project. His obvious pleasure—even arrogance—felt familiar. I was looking into a distorted mirror at my own naïveté. But the mirror showed more: the similarity in our faces. Like mine, his revealed a native genealogy. I could see it in our shared cheekbones, our hair. Suddenly, at that moment, I was hit by the clarity I sought.

The ladder I had climbed was the wrong one.

Distraught, I looked past Alain to his servants standing in silence behind him, two at each side, like four columns of ancestral patience, waiting for the minimal order from their boss. They did not simply have Indian *traits;* they were fully Native American. Their presence, like the gaze of Mayas, Incas, and Aztecs I had met during my travels for the project, evoked profound sadness in me. In the countries I visited, I found Native people living in crushing poverty, sometimes dressed in garish costumes to attract tourists, often crowding city streets, selling Tinkertoy crafts seemingly manufactured in Taiwan. These were the people the project was supposed to help.

I should know better, I thought. The corruption and disorder in Latin America made it difficult for any real change to be imposed from the outside, from the top down—like from my project. Developing factories and services similar to those of the so-called First World had produced nothing but debt and pain in the Third World. The adequacy of this model of development was negated by the facts, both in the reports of social scientists and in the situation on the ground.

That night I was forced to confront the non-sense of my work. That night the Native people at Alain's home, absurdly dressed as English maids, chased my conscience, like spirits of the past asking for revenge from centuries of betrayal. Native people—my people—had been victims of colonials, neocolonials, and even international development specialists with good intentions. The project, like thousands of others aimed at helping the poor, would likely benefit only bankers, Euro-American companies, and corrupt politicians of Latin America.

Until that night, this was the dance I was dancing.

The evening's strange elixir of ocean, tropical sensuality, and unbearable sadness helped me to realize I was not at an elegant party but rather a masquerade ball. Like Cinderella, my childhood heroine, I had made it to the palace. Like her, I now needed to run away. Upon leaving Alain's villa just after midnight, I knew the dance was over for me.

With the same tenacity with which I had walked the Cinderella path, I now escaped it. At the height of my career I left prestige, money, and security. I looked for better ways to serve my people, a different approach to meeting the needs of my community. Using the experience I had gained building my firm, I began a new company. Our approach is based not on profit, but on love and respect. Our core philosophy is not to expand and exploit, but to promote humane change—this time starting from the grassroots level.

The Native woman in me, the one I had hidden from myself as I climbed to the top, was now free. My sadness vanished.

iris stammberger (iris@irisstammberger.com / www.irisstammberger.com) writes and teaches about creativity, innovation, and leadership in the Boston area. Her teachings are inspired by the legends and myths of Native American communities.

∞

Committing to Motherhood

rebecca walker

"Askia, would you like to come over to play after school?"

"I don't know if I can; I'll have to ask my mom."

I hear my son's voice over the bustle of other children and parents gathering coats and lunchboxes. Warmth spreads through me at hearing myself named so easily, so naturally, as one of his "moms." I have been Askia's parent for almost four years now, and yet I am still amazed at how quickly and intuitively I fell in love with this child and accepted a role for myself I never thought I would have—or even want.

When Bashir and I first started seeing each other, she was living in Los Angeles and I was still in New York. With all those flight hours between us, the fact that she had a seven-year-old son didn't seem that big a deal to me. I certainly didn't see myself as one of Askia's parents. But after a year, when we moved in together, I suddenly realized that mother and son were a package deal. And, to put it bluntly, I was terrified. *Me, give up my vagabond lifestyle, be responsible to a child day in and day out?* I mean, I knew I was in love, but was I really *that* in love?

I was never one of those people who thought of having kids as a "when" or even an "if" in my future. I hated it when older relatives such as my stepmother asked when I was going to settle down and have a family. "I'm not sure that's going to happen," I'd reply, before changing the subject. I knew from an early age that I had a nomadic heart, a need for the drama of moving from place to place. Since I turned eighteen, I had moved several times, leaving San Francisco for my first solo apartment in New Haven, my godmother's living room in Manhattan, a mud room with no electricity in Kenya, a studio with no air-conditioning in sweltering Los Angeles . . . I loved being constantly in motion, just as my own family was during my childhood. Then, suddenly, all that came to an end.

In the early days of living with Bashir and Askia, I worried that all my fears would come true: that I was giving up a fundamental part of myself, sacrificing my free spirit to the demands of motherhood like so many women before me. But after a while I could see it wasn't like that. Instead of a huge, mysterious gulf that swallowed me up, I found being a parent was made up of very small and ordinary things: Askia needed someone to drive him to school, to make his lunch, to listen to him talk about how it feels when someone teases him, to read him a story at night. And in living this everyday, drama-free existence, I discovered the bedrock inside myself, the strong self who had learned to find her own stability to survive a life of motion and change.

"What do you want to read tonight," I'd ask. I wanted to share with Askia the books I'd loved as a kid, like *Harriet the Spy* and novels by Judy Blume. But that first year, the books Askia wanted to read horrified me.

"Animorphs!"

I'd sigh and grimace and stall and finally pull one of the blue books off the shelf.

From the beginning, it was important to me to make a full commitment to being a partner and coparent, rather than trying to leave room for a quick exit, should it become necessary, by telling Askia I was a "friend" or "aunt." I knew Askia would eventually have to field questions about his queer parents, and so I wanted to be very clear that I *was* his parent, and that his family was just as stable, strong, and normal as anyone else's.

Fortunately, Askia has not yet encountered any superobvious or in-your-face homophobic reactions to his parents; it hasn't seemed to matter much that he has two moms. Like all kids with same-sex parents, though, Askia did have to figure out what to call me, the nonbiological parent. In the beginning, he called me "Rebecca," which felt safe and neutral for both of us. Then, a couple of years later, Askia looked up at me across the breakfast table and asked, "Can I call you Mom?"

Taken by surprise, I answered without really thinking about it. "Sure, honey, if you want to."

"Okay," he replied, picking up his spoon and digging into his Cheerios. "Thanks, Mom."

It didn't stick though, he already had someone he called Mom. We tried a few other variations—Mommy, Mama—but ended up sticking with the tried-and-true "Rebecca." Still, some of the sweetest moments for me are when I overhear my son calling me his "mom" to one of his friends or teachers. This act of naming makes it clear, as nothing else could, that Askia accepts and knows me unconditionally as one of his parents, one of the people who is there for him 24/7, no matter what. Feeling his confidence in me has helped me realize that despite my parents' divorce and our frequent moves, I always knew they were there for me, too. And so, in parenting, I have finally healed some lingering resentment about my own unsettled childhood.

Now that he's eleven, Askia doesn't always need to hear a story at night, but we still love to read together. Now we just have separate books! We lie in his moms' big bed, me reading the *New Yorker* and him reading *Harry Potter*. If it's close to bedtime, after a few minutes I can see the sleep entering his body; his breathing slows down and the book falls out of his hands. Before he falls too deep, I wake him up and walk him to his own bed for a tuck-in. After he is under the covers, I take his glasses off and kiss his forehead goodnight. I can't help but be amazed that this beautiful child, so present, so right in front of me, is my own.

rebecca walker (www.rebeccawalker.com) frequently speaks on college campuses about Third Wave feminism and multiracial identity. Her books include *To Be Real: Telling the Truth and Changing the Face of Feminism* (Anchor Books) and a memoir, *Black White and Jewish: Autobiography of a Shifting Self* (Riverhead Books). Once in a while, after Askia dozes off, Rebecca has been known to put down the *New Yorker* and read *Harry Potter* late into the night.

∞

Returning Home
wilma mankiller

In the mid-1970s, my two daughters, Felicia and Gina, and I were living in East Oakland, California. At the time I was working at the Native American Youth Center. We could not afford our own place, so we shared a house with another indigenous woman and her child. It was a tough neighborhood. When Felicia's best friend, an eleven-year-old boy, killed himself, I knew it was time to return to my family land in Oklahoma.

I had left my homeland in 1956, when I was ten. That was when my family experienced the pain of the United States government relocation. Our poverty had prompted the move. I recall hearing at that time that the relocation program was being offered as a wonderful opportunity for Indian families to get great jobs, obtain good educations for their kids, and, once and for all, leave poverty behind. In truth, the program gave the government the perfect chance to take Indian people away from their culture and land. The government methods had softened since the nineteenth century, but the end result was the same for native people. Instead of guns and bayonets, the government's Bureau of Indian Affairs used promotional brochures showing staged photographs of smiling Indians in "happy homes" in the big cities.

I never liked the idea of our moving away. I can still remember hiding in a bedroom in our house, listening while my father, mother, and oldest brother talked in the adjoining room about the benefits and drawbacks of relocating our family. Finally, my parents chose San Francisco.

Neon lights, flashily dressed prostitutes, broken glass on the streets, people sleeping in doorways, hard-faced men wandering around. The noises of the city, especially at night, were bewildering. We had left behind the sounds of roosters, dogs, coyotes, bobcats, owls, and crickets moving through the woods. Now we heard traffic. The police and ambulance sirens were the worst. That very first night in the big city, we were all huddled under the covers. We had never heard sirens before. I thought it was some sort of wild creature screaming.

The overt discrimination we encountered is what got to me the most. It became obvious that ethnic intolerance was a fact of life in California, even in the urbane and sophisticated world of San Francisco. Not only did African and Hispanic Americans feel the sting of racism, so did native Americans. A popular sign in restaurants in the 1950s read NO DOGS, NO INDIANS.

The "better life" the BIA had promised all of us was, in reality, life in a tough, urban ghetto. Many native people were unable to find jobs. Many endured a great deal of poverty, emotional suffering, substance abuse, and poor health because of leaving their homelands, families, and communities. They were exiles living far from their native lands. Urban Indian families banded together, built Indian centers, held picnics and powwows, and tried to form communities in the midst of large urban populations. Yet there was always and forever a persistent longing to go home.

Many families we met there were like us. They had come to the realization that the BIA's promises were empty. We all seemed to have reached that same terrible conclusion—the government's relocation program was a disaster that robbed us of our vitality and sense of place.

Although thousands of American Indians had been relocated, the relocation act's goal of abolishing ties to tribal lands was never realized—thank goodness. Our traditional people would not abide by this federal interference. They continued grassroots efforts to unify the Cherokees and to resist the initiatives of the federal government to bring about total assimilation of the Cherokee people. A large percentage of native people who had been removed to urban areas ultimately moved back to their original homes.

Now a single mom with kids of my own, more and more, I found my eyes, too, turning away from the sea and the setting sun. I looked to the east, where the sun begins its daily journey. That was where I had to go . . . back to the land of my birth, back to the soil and trees my grandfather had touched, back to the animals and birds whose calls I had memorized as a girl when we packed our things and left on a westbound train so very long ago. The circle had to be completed. It was so simple, so easy.

I was going home.

After the sad suicide of Felicia's friend, and without any idea of where I would work and just enough money to get to Oklahoma, we rented a U-Haul truck, packed all our belongings, and headed across country accompanied by our dog, a guinea pig, and lunches packed by our friends. We covered some of the same territory my family had traveled across twenty years before when we had been relocated by the federal government. When we arrived at my mother's place, I had $20 to my name, no car, no job, and few, if any, prospects. But we were happy. We stored our belongings and stayed with relatives in a house without indoor plumbing. Quite a change from Oakland! In some ways, it must have been as strange for my daughters as when I went to San Francisco as a child. The girls had had some experience getting along with few amenities . . . but they were not prepared for such living on a daily basis.

At first, I had a difficult time getting a position. Whenever I went to the tribal headquarters to inquire about the various jobs being advertised, I was told that I was overqualified or, for some reason, just did not fit. Finally, I got fed up with hearing that, so I went right into the office and said, "I want to work! Whatever you have, please let me try it. I need to work!" Apparently that approach was effective. I got a low-level management job with the Cherokee Nation. At last I was home to stay.

wilma mankiller started her job at a time when there were no female executives at the Cherokee Nation, and there had never been an elected female deputy or principal chief. Six years later *she* was elected the first female Deputy Principal Chief of the Cherokee Nation—and four years after that, she was elected to be the first female Principal Chief of this second-largest Native American Nation in the United States. This story contains both original material and adapted excerpts from *Mankiller: A Chief and Her People* by Wilma Mankiller and Michael Wallis. Copyright © 1993 by Wilma Mankiller and Michael Wallis. Reprinted by permission of St. Martin's Press, LLC.

∞

Courage at the End
mireya herrera

"Mireya, pienso que llegó la hora. I think it's almost time," she said.

"Yo sé. I know," I nodded, taking her thin hand.

"What will I say to them?" Her fingers squeezed around mine.

"What do you want to say? What do you need to say?" I asked. My throat tightened and I wondered, like always, what *I* could say that would help *her. Por favor, Dios, help me to guide her.*

The hospital room was so sterile, so cold. It smelled of disinfectant. No place to die. No place to say good-bye, to say last loving words, the most important words ever needed to be said, to three little kids about to begin such a difficult journey. They were about to be left to live their lives—their childhoods, adolescence, adulthoods—motherless.

"I won't see them at their proms, or driving their first cars," Lisa cried.

"I know." I blinked. How long before my own tears flowed? How much of a professional distance did I need to maintain? I could cry later, on the way home, if I needed to. That always helped; a necessary release.

I am a social worker who for ten years has been leading support groups for women who are HIV positive or have AIDS. One of the hardest parts of my work, the thing that takes the most strength and compassion, is when a woman is at the end of her life and she asks me to help her find a way to say good-bye to her children.

Lisa (not her real name) was Latina, in her thirties, and mother of three—ages eleven, seven, and four. She had been in the hospital a lot during the last few months, so her ex-husband and her mother were caring for the kids. I had known Lisa for three years and we weren't especially close, but she had attended my support group. Our primary contact now was by phone. She called during moments of anguish and distress. One evening she called from the hospital and asked me to come in.

"Mireya, it's time," she said. Over the years I have found that the women I work with can often tell when they are close to dying. "My kids, Mireya. I haven't done enough. There's so much I haven't said to them. I haven't told them what I want them to know, about everything, I mean," she wept.

What could I possibly say to this woman to ease her mind?

I just encouraged her to talk. I asked her what it was she felt she had not done, and what she needed to do to get it done. As she spoke, it became clear it wasn't so much that she had specific things she needed to do or say, it was just that she was having a hard time letting go. She needed reassurance that her children would be okay without her. Unfortunately, this was something I could not—no one could—give her.

Finally I told her: "It's okay to let go, to die. You have done all you can."

Ultimately, this is what dying mothers need to hear. I have had to say these words to more than a dozen.

Some want to know *exactly* how to say good-bye to their kids, but again, these things can't be scripted by others. So Lisa and I discussed together how she would tell her children that she was going to die now—that she would be gone from their (physical) lives forever. She decided to hold each child and say, "Remember that I love you, always. Even though I am not here."

When women ask, I pray with them. Sometimes I shed tears with them. I try to stay in my social worker role, but in order to remain present, truly present, I occasionally have to cry as we talk. Now that I am a parent, too, I can't help thinking about my own little boy and what his life would be like without me.

I feel sad but also confident when I finally say to a woman, "It's okay to let go." Somehow I manage to say it with total certainty, because these women *are* ready to die. They're just waiting for somebody to speak the words that will allow them to move on.

It's hard to explain how I have been able to do this work day in and day out for ten years. The original commitment I made to the work was strong. It transformed me personally and spiritually. And even with the hardships that can sometimes come, in the past decade I have never once questioned my initial decision. I know this is what I was put here to do. The best I can say is that God has given me the ability and the courage to be with women at the end of their lives.

mireya herrera, a licensed clinical social worker in Sacramento, California, finds that talking and crying about difficulties helps heal the pain. She loves her work and feels privileged and honored to be a part of many women's end-of-life processes. As it is a time of emotional and spiritual growth for all involved, Mireya thanks the women she works with for enriching her own life.

CHAPTER 3

For Ourselves: Taking Charge of Our Bodies and Sexuality

On their own terms

AT THEIR OWN INITIATIVE

With whomever they choose

Finally, women and girls can define their own sexuality. They are able to say no when they want to say no, yes when they want to say yes, *and* do the asking—leaving it to the cutie they spot on the other side of the room to respond.

Historically, women's bodies have been a real site of oppression—from sexual assault and inadequate health care (including restrictions on reproductive choice) to being told how to act, how to dress, whom to love. Make no mistake: The battle isn't over yet. But during the past few decades there's been a revolution regarding women taking an active role in sexual matters.

Traditional norms dictated that a woman be modest. She was the leg-crossing, no-saying figure who was the main obstacle to a sex act. When she finally did get sexual (after incessant pressure), it was always with a man, never a woman, and she was to react and respond, never instigate. It took guts to be an openly desiring female because being a sexual girl meant being a bad girl. She'd be discounted, ostracized. No longer "pure," she'd fall on the other end of the spectrum labeled "slut."

These traditional norms are still present in some women's lives. But now the norms have morphed into a confusing mixed message, because in today's multimedia-based culture the so-called slut is actually promoted (though in real life she is still punished). She is the scantily clad, *just-do-me*-looking, hypersexualized young woman revered in ads, movies, magazines, and music videos. No longer the obstacle to sex, today's girls and women are supposed to personify it; according to the media images, they are to look attractive, lusty, and be sexually available at all times for the men of the world. Women have learned to accept being on constant display. Worse, what is considered attractive is defined for them by the fashion and media industries. A woman's value depends on whether her looks meet the industries' definition—and how much male attention she gets.

From women being told they are not supposed to be sexual, to being told they should be more sexual, our sexuality has been played like a Ping-Pong ball in a game of table tennis. So the truth is worth repeating: A woman's body is her body, and it shouldn't be pushed around by anybody else. We all need to be in command of our own selves. We all need to make our own sexual decisions.

That is what the women and girls in this chapter are doing. They break the bounds of both the older and newer norms. They do this by choosing for themselves. They have the courage to revel in their sexiness, uncross their legs, and instigate erotic acts—at their own initiative, on their own terms, and with whomever they choose. And they also adamantly refuse to let others see or use them as sex objects when they don't particularly feel like being one. They are redefining for themselves (and us!) the concepts of beauty, sexuality, and what is considered an acceptable loving relationship. These women-on-top are taking charge.

Cupid's Paintbrush
amelia copeland

I'm being sullen, bitchy, and a really bad sport. *Who talked me into this anyway?* It's 7:00 in the morning and I'm watching four thousand shiny, happy people doing jumping jacks in the park. I seem to be one of the few who have avoided the contagion of this touching community spirit, this thousand-points-of-light, or whatever it's called these days. It's our citywide, one-day-a-year volunteering event, and all I can think is, "If any one of you spills my coffee, if any one of you even threatens to touch my coffee, the carnage begins." That's my community spirit.

Actually, I do know why I'm here. I'm sick of my life. I want to meet new people. It's just my luck they put me in a group with an entire fraternity of business-school students. Thanks. Thanks very much.

Eventually they send us off to paint the office of a housing project. And I admit that as I start to paint, I'm getting into it. There's a kind of Zen to dipping the paintbrush in the can just deep enough, then sliding it across a window sash, holding it at the perfect angle so it passes smoothly along the edge of the pane without touching it. They're blasting the radio, and even though the music sucks, it's appropriate for this activity: "Shiny happy people, shiny happy people painting, shiny happy people painting walls . . . "

There's one guy here who seems a little different from the others—pleasant, good-natured, with a functional mind and a healthy distaste for venture capital and investment banking. I talk to him for a few minutes during lunch and try to muster up some sexual interest just for the heck of it, but he's a bit too tall and gawky for me. Still, he does have kind of a nice mouth.

As the afternoon wears on, the shiny people start to lose interest in their well-meaning community ideals, leaving their paintbrushes to atrophy in the trays. They sit around gabbing about stocks and bonds. I'm still caught up in the meditative

72

aspects of painting, so when the job is done and all the masking tape peeled away, I'm not quite ready to go. I start collecting the brushes and trays left by my spoiled coworkers.

As I'm walking around gathering tools, I run across my friend from lunch, who has donned a bandanna to keep the paint out of his hair. I don't know why, but a little bell goes off in my head and my internal Cupid—or Dionysus more likely—says, "Hey, this guy looks kinda cute with that thing on his head." Uh-oh.

I take the brushes and trays into the bathroom at the end of the hall. Starting to wash the brushes one by one in the sink, I try not to get paint all over myself, but it's hopeless. So I dump everything in the tub, turn up the water, and plunge my hands wrist-deep into the mass of gloppy paint. Running my fingers between the brush bristles I develop a true appreciation for the texture of latex: smooth and viscous, it slides over my hands like a skin of wet silk. The bandanna guy is still nestled in my mind somewhere and there is a tension building between the thought of him still working down the hall and the feeling of slippery paint on my skin. Quickly, I rinse my hands off and bolt out of the bathroom. Now I'm on a mission.

I look in each of the rooms to the right and left of the hallway, but I don't see him. The idea is firmly planted in my head now, and if I don't find him, or if he resists me, I don't know what I'm going to do. When I get down to the end of the hall and there's only one room left, I turn the corner. *Okay. There he is.* I'm ignoring every shoot of trepidation, though they're sprouting faster and faster. *Keep moving,* I tell myself as I stride over to him.

"You're not shy are you?" I say.

"Uh, no, I don't think so."

"Come with me." I grab his hand and pull him back down the hall. *This is the longest hall I have ever been in.* "Come on, hurry."

We get into the bathroom and I close the door. He is looking at me as if I'm insane, but he's also smiling. I immerse my hands deep in the thick paint in one of the trays and smear it all over my fingers and wrists. Then I grab his hands and work the paint all

73

over them, between his fingers, across his palms and partway up his arms. He's grinning at me as his fingers start to move, smoothing and kneading the paint into my hands. We step closer and he envelops my mouth with his. Our tongues explore and slip around each other as our fingers slide and entangle. Hurriedly, I undo his shirt buttons, take more paint into my hands, then smear it over his chest. He slides my shirt up, pushing my bra above my breasts, and we crush against each other, rubbing and smearing the slippery paint all over ourselves. He reaches to get a handful of paint and massages it smoothly onto my breasts. I bite his lower lip just as there's a banging on the door: "Anyone in there?" We freeze, on the edge of bursting out laughing.

"Yeah, just a minute."

We lunge at each other's mouths, and with them glued together, try to adjust our clothing over our sticky skin and the drying layer of paint on our chests. Now we are laughing, trying to maintain as much oral contact as we can while turning the taps on full blast and washing our own and each other's hands. We straighten out, step back from each other, and look down at our bodies, shaking our heads. We're a mess. Our clothes are stuck onto us rakishly and there's paint all over them. "Oh well," he shrugs, and I open the door. We walk out as nonchalantly as we can manage under the gaping stares of the future masters of industry.

amelia copeland (am@paramour.com) is the former editor of *Paramour* magazine, Lustrologist for the *Boston* and *Providence Phoenix* adult sections, and a working stiff. Her story in this collection was just the beginning of her wild years.

∞

Smutmonger
cecilia tan

*Nimble fingers played over my sides, enticing me to turn over as he searched
my stomach and my throat and my thighs for soft places. And then the kisses
began, under my chin, on my forehead, my eyelids, my lips. As he broke
away I looked up into his eyes . . .*

My parents' backyard in the suburbs is big enough to fit a tennis
court and a swimming pool. Fortunately, they never built either
one, which meant that one summer night in 1998 there was
plenty of space for a big yellow and white striped tent, tables and
chairs for about a hundred people, and a small tent just for me,
The Author, to sit under and autograph copies of my book. A
book of erotica. That night I signed a copy of the book for my
godmother, my uncle, my mother's tennis instructor. It wasn't a
place I had really expected to end up.

I started writing about sex when I was a teenager, when I
dreamed of being a writer, and also, well, some other things adolescent girls dream about. I wrote sexy stories about celebrities,
weird sci-fi tales of procreating aliens, and hormone-ridden
scenes involving people I had crushes on. I never showed them to
anyone. At the time, I figured I'd grow up to write something
"respectable" and socially acceptable, like science fiction or literary fiction, and that all the sex stories were just a phase I was going
through. I knew many people in society would consider erotic
fantasies to be the least important of all possible topics I could
explore in my writing, and some would outright condemn it.

Through college I concentrated on literary topics, but after I
graduated and went out into the world, I found myself going
back toward those old erotic fantasies. I tried to write some
"conventional" fiction; it mostly sat unfinished on my computer.
It wasn't until I went back to writing erotic stories that I caught
fire, that I felt as if I was writing something worth reading. This
time I did show the stories to people. I shared them with friends
and lovers, and on the Internet. These erotic pieces were the first

stories that I had accepted for publication, that were praised in reviews, and that I felt made a difference in the world.

That's when I took a risk and self-published a small collection of my stories dealing with erotic power exchange and role-playing. Even though I identified as a feminist, set my stories on a faraway planet (yup, still hooked on sci-fi), and gave my characters pure-hearted motivations, I was still afraid that people who read the stories would condemn them as antifeminist. I was worried about one feminist in particular, my mom, who had raised me to value equality and freedom, and who I thought might be a bit shocked to read my work. I waited eight months before giving her a copy of the book. At first, I was right; she was a little shocked. But once she understood the concept of erotic role-playing, she agreed with me that both it and erotic fantasy are about building an intimate and special bond between loving partners, and not about oppressing people or infringing on their rights—and certainly not about exploiting women.

One of the early decisions I made was to publish my erotic fiction under my real name. I was proud of my work and wanted to use it to promote a more sex-positive worldview. I wanted to plant the seeds in people's imaginations that it was okay to want some variation in their sex lives, that it was okay to explore bisexuality, role-playing, sex toys, and the like, and most of all that it was okay to fantasize. I didn't feel I could stand up and advocate that people be more honest with themselves about their desires if I myself were hiding. So for the past decade, with my real name, I've published all along the ideological spectrum, from *Ms.* magazine to *Penthouse*. The result is that ever since showing my mom my self-published collection of stories, I have been "out" to all my family and friends about what I do. Now, being "out" as a sex writer is one thing; autographing seventy-five copies of your book of erotica for cousins, childhood neighbors, and your mom's chiropractor is another. But when my first major book came out from a big publisher, my mom wanted to throw a book-launch party for me; so that's how we came to have a big striped tent in the backyard, a live jazz combo, and a dining-room table turned catering station. I figured most of the guests would never even look in the book. Then, halfway through the party, Mom sidled up to me and whispered, "Everyone's waiting to hear you read."

Oh. I'd done hundreds of readings at that point, at bookstores, at open mikes, on the radio, at conventions. It's different somehow when people who have known you since you were five are sitting out there, fanning themselves with copies of the book, and smiling proudly at you. I began frantically skimming the table of contents to find a story I could read. *Is there a story in here,* I wondered, *that was funny, not too long, and didn't have anything too extreme?* There was.

Mosquitoes buzzing around the electric lights hung in the tent, I stepped up in front of the group and opened the book.

> *I felt something hard but gentle draw a line down the seam of my jeans, the motorcycle's ignition key in her hand, now pointing at that spot where I could feel it most. We didn't talk after that.*

cecilia tan (www.ceciliatan.com), who lives in the Boston area, is the author of *Black Feathers* (HarperCollins) and the founder and editor of pioneering erotica publisher Circlet Press (www.circlet.com; "Books Celebrating Sexuality & The Erotic Mind"). She also teaches tae kwon do and erotic writing workshops—though not at the same time.

∞

Big Beauty ✳
tess dehoog

When I was feeling especially brave one day, I bought a tank top. Being a fat girl pretty much my entire life, I wasn't good at wearing clothes that were tight-fitting or revealed a lot of skin. Then one day, it was boiling hot outside. I didn't own many light summer things, so I headed to the local fat-lady clothing store.

It was not a very hip store, though basic things like tee shirts were easy to find there, and that was what was on my agenda, considering the heat. As usual, I found all the tee shirts I needed, but for some reason I kept wandering back to the rack with the tank tops. The saleswoman caught me eyeing them. She encouraged me to try one on. "Why cover what you can't hide," she said, and I couldn't argue with such wisdom.

Inside the dressing room, looking in the mirror, all I saw was the tire around my belly and the flab on my arms. I stared for a while, then decided I might never be brave enough to try it on again and I didn't want to lose what could be my last chance, so I bought it. *Plus,* I further convinced myself, *no one looks good under fluorescent lights.*

I brought the shirt home where it sat in my closet for a few weeks. Sometimes I tried it on but it never left the apartment. Then I went on a trip and brought the tank top along with me. I hoped to work up the nerve to wear it in a city I didn't live in and where I wouldn't have to see anyone I met there ever again.

Finally, the day arrived. I wore my tank top outside.

No one looked at me strangely. No one stared and the world did not stop. I didn't hear a single laugh or snicker. I felt so good and brave, I didn't care that only the bottom half of my arms were tanned. The first day I wore my tank top I went to a fair. The tops of my arms had never seen bumper cars before. It was awesome to feel so free. I felt naked and even a little sexy.

I love what my tank top has done for me and what I have done for my tank top. My tank top makes me feel more comfortable about my body, more beautiful. And I've taken a flat, boring tank top and filled it out quite nicely.

tess dehoog (tess@vcn.bc.ca) is a sexy, fat girl from Vancouver, Canada. She's young, pretty, and intends to make every fat person in the world love his or her body.

∞

First Pride
amanda rivera

Today was the big day, and me and my mom Ingrid led the way. She said there were almost two hundred marchers. Along the road, people were holding up signs saying JESUS OR HELL and NO PLACE FOR DYKES. But there were also people holding up other signs saying THEY'RE PEOPLE, TOO. Besides, we had police to protect us.

Meanwhile, my other mom, Shantal, was walking around, talking, and checking if people were okay. The marchers looked excited and proud. I felt that they were proud of who they were, and so was I. Later we went out for pizza!

This was the first Gay Pride march in my town of Lawrence, Massachusetts.

amanda rivera was eight years old and in the third grade when she wrote this. She is Puerto Rican/African-American and enjoys "reading, writing, riding my bike, and playing board games with my mommies." Amanda hates unfairness in the world and pollution. She can be contacted via her mom (lesbymom@yahoo.com).

∞

Loving w/o Limits
robin renée

Late one Sunday night, I came home from a music conference exhausted and looking forward to a solid night's rest. However, as a borderline Internet junkie, I was compelled to the computer to check my e-mail. There I found a message from a friend in Canada saying she had read an announcement that Black Entertainment Television (BET) was looking for an African-American woman to discuss polyamory on a talk show. It was *BET Tonight,* hosted by Tavis Smiley. They wanted someone the very next night.

My initial response: *Me? A live talk show? No edits? No way.*

I imagined a rabid TV audience yelling at me, calling out, "Useless slut!" I didn't trust myself to speak with clarity in the face of that, in a setting where there would be no changes, no takebacks. Besides, I just didn't want to. I was weary from having been elected the unofficial sex/relationship/poly counselor and educator of my social circle. The last thing I wanted was to become the National Polyamory Poster Child. I went to bed knowing it wasn't going to happen.

My subconscious must have had other ideas, because I tossed and turned all night. When morning came, I called.

I left a message for the show's producer at 11:30 A.M. She called back within the hour. There would be no rabid television audience, she said—no live audience at all, just two other guests and a few phone callers. It was to be a balanced, intelligent discussion on the topic of—I still laugh at her term—"mansharing." By 3:15 that same afternoon, a car arrived at my house to take me to the airport. By 5:30 I was on a plane headed for Washington, D.C., and my first national television appearance.

The set design attempted to hint at living-room ease, but the *BET Tonight* logo was displayed so prominently, the stiffness of television land could not be forgotten. I was seated next to one guest, a perfectly placed cup of water in front of each of us. The second guest appeared on a TV monitor via satellite. We watched as she readied herself in San Francisco. Our host was whisked in at the last moment before broadcast and quickly seated across from me.

Earlier, the producer had informed me that the two guests I'd be speaking with were "experts," one in favor of open relationships, the other against. She was almost right. I was left to converse with two experts who held exactly the same opinion: Women who "share their men" are insecure, confused women who don't know the potential for depth, security, and connection in a one-on-one relationship. The two Expert Relationship Therapists talked at length about "mansharing" in terms of lying, cheating, and deceit, clandestine phone calls and hidden rendezvous behind other women's backs. They spoke of it as a situation that only a weak woman with no alternative would accept. They had little concept of a woman who might love more than one partner, of relationships based on complete openness, spiritual love, and balance.

I stayed relatively calm, more so than I had anticipated. I chose not to take the defensive, or to approach the discussion as if it were a debate. In fact, I was surprisingly levelheaded and articulate, given that it was live TV. I talked in general terms about my innate understanding of sexuality as a beautiful experience that may be expressed in a myriad of healthy ways. And I spoke specifically about my experience with Keith, whom I have loved since college. We have had a powerful, dynamic, more-than-ten-year relationship, while simultaneously having other important loves as well. It worked for us. Everyone involved was happy. We respected each other, met each other's needs, and kept the whole thing remarkably real, loving, and honest. Keith and his live-in girlfriend knew I was going on BET, and they were cool with that.

The show, meanwhile, was a subtle comedy of miscommunication, an understated *Who's On First?*

Host: "If I hear what the experts are saying, you are in denial, you have a maturity problem . . . yet you decide to put your face all over television. Let me ask you, why are you okay with a mansharing relationship?"

Me: "Honestly, I feel I'm more than okay with it; it's natural for me to be in a state of openness in my relationships."

Expert #1: "I think you can glamorize that you have commitmentphobia, or other issues, so that even *you* believe you know what you're doing."

Expert #2: "There is a price to be paid when you are subjected to the abuse of mansharing, and the price for most women is their self-esteem."

Host: "Some make the argument that women are involved in this because there is a shortage of available men. Your thoughts?"

Me: "No, it's something very different from that. This is the organic development of my way of loving."

Expert #1: "What do you mean by *organic*?"

Host: "Do you maybe stay with your man because he takes you out, buys you nice things?"

Though it seems we missed talking to each other (and even about the same topic) by quite some margin, I believe we all accomplished what we set out to do. *BET Tonight* aired a show on a controversial topic that doubtless did well in the ratings. The therapists expressed their opinions and plugged their books heavily. I had the opportunity to articulate something that is rarely voiced: We have choices, actual choices. We can live according to our inner guidance. We can love fully and completely without limitations imposed on us by others.

The final statement by one of the therapists, paraphrased, was, "If you're sharing your man, you only have a piece of the pie." I say this: Our emotional/sexual/romantic selves are not pie graphs. By loving, we are not divided, nor are we diminished. To give to one, to give to more, cannot deplete something eternal.

robin renée (www.robinrenee.com) is a poly/ bi/ Wiccan/ Buddhist/ mystic/ singer/ songwriter/ poet/ activist/ writer in the Philadelphia area. From her earliest relationships, she has always loved freely and openly.

∞

Good, Good, Good, Good Vibrations
joani blank

The bell over the door chimes as a woman enters. She's in her midthirties and dressed in a neat button-up blouse. When she approaches the counter, where I'm busily hand-stamping the words PLAIN BROWN WRAPPER on a stack of grocery bags, she speaks quietly, so no one else can hear: "I'd like to buy a . . . a *vibrator,* please."

My eyes meet hers, then turn to the shelves that line the tiny room I call my store. She follows my gaze and we laugh at the same time. "I guess that's about all you sell here, isn't it?" she says in a relieved tone.

"Yup," I answer, smiling broadly.

I didn't set out to open the first women-oriented sex-toy store in the country, but in 1977, I wasn't that surprised to find myself doing it either. I'd worked with the Sex Counseling Program at the University of California at San Francisco for several years. Much of my work was simply teaching women to have orgasms through masturbation, so naturally vibrators were an important part of our conversations. But it was difficult for my clients to make the leap from discussing vibrators to actually *getting hold* of a real live one to try. At that time, women's only choices were to order sex toys "sight unseen" from a men's catalogue or to visit an "adult store."

Usually located in seamy parts of town, these stores were run and patronized by men. The only women appeared in lurid pictures on the covers of porn videos lining the walls. Even when women from my groups braved this sexist atmosphere, their gutsiness was often met with more intimidation. When one of my clients asked a store clerk if she could examine a vibrator under the glass countertop, he leered in response, "Boy, you must need it bad, lady."

After I heard that story, I complained to a feminist colleague who was known for her innovative and bold actions: "Toni, you should open a vibrator store for women."

"Too busy," my friend characteristically replied. "You do it."

It made sense. I had recently left my job as a sex counselor, and my living expenses were low enough that I could afford to run a store that just broke even for a while. With full knowledge of the fact that most new businesses folded within a year, I scraped together enough to rent a little storefront on the edge of upscale, family-oriented Noe Valley, and plunged into the risky world of a small business owner. I ordered vibrators from wholesalers and placed a few discreet ads in the local paper, calling my shop *Good Vibrations:* "A vibrator store and museum, especially but not exclusively for women." I bought brown paper bags without our name on it, so folks could hide their purchases if they wanted (but for fun we stamped PLAIN BROWN WRAPPER on each bag). I even put together a catalogue—a crummy little mimeographed fold-over sheet featuring two plug-in vibrators, two battery-operated ones, and a few books: *Our Bodies, Ourselves; For Yourself* (a masturbation handbook); and the sex workbooks I had written, *A Playbook for Women about Sex,* and a similar one for men, both published by my own outfit, Down There Press (get it?).

My mission was simple: to encourage women to take charge of and have fun with their sexuality; this in a society that deemed nonsexual women pure and good, and sexual women tramps. I also advocated that men be full partners as their women lovers explored and experienced their sexuality. I planned to exploit people's interest in sex rather than their anxiety about it.

When I opened the store, I never considered, "What will people think?" I was married at the time, and my father-in-law *did* seem rather confused about what I was doing. ("What exactly are you selling, Joani?" he asked at one family gathering. "Vacuum cleaners?") But the vast majority of reactions, from friends and strangers, were supportive or curious.

"And what do you do?"

"I sell vibrators."

"Oh." Pause. "I see." Extended pause. "Great! How's business?"

Perhaps my bold move did not meet with much resistance because San Francisco in the 1970s was a place of sexual freedom and feminist consciousness-raising. The attitude was "anything goes"—though to protect the privacy of our customers, we placed curtains in the storefront window. What modesty we did have took the form of keeping a few realistic-looking dildos in a wooden cabinet, which customers had to inquire to see. People would look all around and then ask "Do you have anything else?" and I knew that meant dildos.

From the beginning, the store attracted a wide range of customers, from heterosexuals who heard about us through the grapevine to lesbian couples who lived in the area. Lots of men, eager to learn about sex from a woman's perspective, came in alone, too. I admit, I got a certain perverse pleasure out of talking with customers about "shocking" things, like dildos and masturbation, in a no-nonsense, straightforward way. And it was a relief for others to realize they could talk about those things. No one I spoke to about my work and mission was so conservative that they couldn't at least respect what I was doing. Most, in fact, sang my praises. Mine was an idea whose time had come. It had been a sexual wasteland for women out there. My clean, well-lighted store, a discreet shop with nice curtains, was an oasis.

One of my favorite memories from those early days is of a man who came in one afternoon when I was the only one working. He walked over to my one little shelf of books and stood in front of it for the longest time, totally still, with just his head moving back and forth looking at the titles. After a while, I started to feel slightly nervous. *Is this guy a creep?* I wondered. We did get those from time to time. Just as I was working up the nerve to ask if I could help, the man turned to face me and said in an awed voice, "I can't believe I've gotten to be thirty-six years old and I obviously still don't know the first thing about sex."

"Well," I responded heartily. "You've come to the right place."

joani blank's San Francisco store did not fold within a year. Instead, it expanded to include a very popular mail-order service and a second location. In an unusual move, Joani (www.joaniblank.com) restructured GV to be a worker-cooperative so that each loyal employee became an equal owner. GV now has close to seventy owners, and grossed close to $10 million last year. You can buy your very own vibrator at www.goodvibes.com.

∞

Declawing Catcalls
julia acevedo

The Saturday after Thanksgiving is a real pain if you're in retail. But there I was, working on the busiest shopping day of the year, and on what was supposed to be my day off, too. It was a bad, *bad* Saturday. I was pushed, shoved, yelled at, and on my feet since opening at 7:00 that morning. By 2:00, I was ready to deck a few halls, not to mention a few surly customers. Stella, my sympathetic manager, took pity and gave me the rest of the day off. I had to relax. I needed coffee.

It was chilly outside and I tugged at the thin sweater I wore and smoothed my skirt against my legs. Stella liked the store tropically warm; anything more than a bikini was overkill. But now that I was outside . . . brrr. I slung my purse over my shoulder and headed for the corner coffee shop. That's when I saw, halfway between me and the café at the other end of the block, the group of men standing in the middle of the sidewalk as if they owned the universe.

These guys were unreal. There were usually a dozen or so of them standing in front of the bar, their home away from home. Within the thirty-five to sixty-five age range, they smoked cigars, talked loudly, guffawed like donkeys, and made wild gestures when they conversed with one another. At work, we called them *"those* guys," and I avoided them whenever I could because, frankly, they were kind of scary. In their dark glasses, shiny suits, and black leather jackets, they looked and sounded like escapees from a Martin Scorsese movie. But, alas for them, because I was *in a mood,* I had to (wanted to!) walk right through them.

As I got closer, I kept my stride even. I was thinking they could probably smell fear. When I was within ten feet, they all stopped talking and turned to stare. The congregation parted like the Red Sea so I could pass, and more than a dozen pairs of eyes burned holes into me. At one point I was surrounded, which was so intimidating because not one of them said a word. I became very conscious of myself and felt awfully small and alone.

I walked the disturbing gauntlet in total silence. After I passed, I heard the *Oooo, babeeeee*'s and kissy-kissy noises start up. One even said, "That is one BEE-YOO-TEE-FULL piece of ass."

Now before I go on, you should know one thing about me: All my life I was taught that "nice" girls never spoke up or voiced an opinion about anything, even things that were bothering them. That was how I was raised. But the last line—that one specific line—was the straw that broke the camel's back. It filled me with a blinding, unstoppable fury that *had* to be released. I'd been taking abuse from harried holiday shoppers all day, and now I had to listen to this crap from these bastards . . . and just let it slide? *Absolutely not.* I stopped in my tracks and turned to face them.

Heated blood surged through my body. I felt my skin flush and my eyes narrow. I planted my feet apart, put my hands on my hips, and asked, "Did one of you assholes just call me a BEE-YOO-TEE-FULL piece of ass?"

They certainly weren't expecting this response. They looked incredibly surprised I had said anything at all.

"How dare you talk to me like that. You don't even know me! What gives you the right to talk to *anyone* like that? How would you feel," I continued, "if someone talked that way to your daughters? Well, I'm somebody's daughter, too, and I demand the same consideration."

I know, it sounds a bit *Thelma-and-Louise*-ish, but I stared them down, daring any one of them to say or do anything. But they didn't. It was as if they were frozen in shock, so I turned to go. I was a bit shaky—standing up to more than a dozen catcalling freaks all by myself was something I would normally never do—but I also felt this incredible rush from what I had just done, and I certainly wasn't cold anymore. The whole thing was strangely exhilarating.

"Hey, wait a minute," said a voice behind me.

I spun around and spat, "Why, did you think of a clever comeback, like 'Nice tits,' maybe?"

I looked at the man who'd spoken: about forty-five, dark eyes, dark hair, black jeans, black leather jacket. *This one probably thinks he's Fonzie,* I thought, and suppressed an amused smile. He raised his hands to his chest in a palms-out gesture and said, "We are sorry we offended you. Some of us don't know how to behave around ladies, see. That stuff you said, you're right. We have no right to say things like that to you, okay? We're sorry we disrespected you."

"You shouldn't disrespect *anyone* like that."

"I know," said Mr. Spokesman-for-the-Group. "And I apologize. We all apologize."

I looked at him over the tops of my sunglasses, and then into the eyes of the silent, nodding others. Now it was *my* turn to be shocked at *their* response. At last I said, "I accept your apology."

Long story short, over the next few months I got to know all of "*those* guys," and they got to know me, and now we are friends. Sometimes they can annoy, but aside from the occasional "doll" or "sweetheart," they have now learned some manners; they call me by my name and give me the respect I deserve. And that is the most important thing.

julia acevedo now believes "nice" girls shouldn't wait for the last straw before they speak their minds. Nice girls have mouths, and they should learn to use them. Early, loudly, and often.

∞

MTV, Bite Me!

sabrina margarita alcantara-tan

"Wanna be part of a rock video?"

I was pretty excited about this call from my casting agency, since the band doing the video was one of the biggest heavy-metal groups in the country and I really liked their music. They needed a bunch of girls to drink beer, get wasted, and essentially trash a house. *Hey, I can do that.*

The next day I dressed in the required gear—'80s rock sleaze—and was driven to a house purchased specifically to be trashed for the video. It was deep in the boonies, a remote area of Brooklyn. In the chilly November air, I joined other extras lined up at the catering booth, got some veggie gumbo, and went to a side tent where power heaters warmed our freezing butts. There, we waited to be called for a scene.

I looked around. Though there were more than a hundred of us, I noticed immediately, and was not surprised, that I was one of only a few women of color. Many extras were in jeans; some wore revealing cutout tops and pants. The more glamorous-looking ones sported leather pants, cowboy hats, and high-heeled boots.

A handful of girls from the shoot the night before had been called back for another day's work. One, a major glam girl with lip gloss slathered on her mouth and her hair teased up, was standing around, so I decided to find out what was happening.

"Hey," I said, "is the band in the house?"

She gave me a haughty look. "No, they were here yesterday. Today it's just the girls."

I was disappointed but still excited.

As the day wore on, lots of us, including me, still weren't called. When we saw a few women coming back after doing scenes, we all crowded around and asked what they had done.

"Did you start wrecking the house?" asked a woman in black suede boots.

"No," answered one of the returning women, looking tired.

89

"We just made out with the other girls and then they sent us back to makeup for more lipstick."

Made out? I was confused, and curious enough to leave the warm tent and brave the cold to check out what was happening in the house.

I saw two mixed-Asian gals standing before a group of white guys. One of the men was yelling and gesturing. Then both women took off their shirts and pressed up against the wall in a tight embrace, kissing. The men ran around filming for a few minutes before waving the women away.

"What was *that* about?" I asked as the women approached me.

"I don't know," answered one. "I guess the director is some famous European dude, and he got this great inspiration yesterday to do a lesbian sex thing for the video."

"Are you okay with it?" I asked.

She looked embarrassed. "I guess," she muttered. "It felt kind of awkward. I didn't really want to do it, but you know . . ." Her voice trailed off.

I found out the video was originally supposed to showcase the band playing in the house with all these women hanging off them, kinda like a whorehouse . . . and it gets better. They'd also had a bunch of hard-looking biker guys, but they were fired when the director experimented with having two women make out, and thus the direction of the video blossomed.

Back in the tent, women who had already done scenes were telling their stories to the rest of the extras. A few looked like they were about to cry.

"It's not just kissing," reported one girl. "They're having us do heavy petting now, like real sex stuff."

Other women nodded and added their two cents.

"They told me we were just going to trash a house."

"Yeah, they told me that, too."

"Where are they going to show this video, anyway? This is soft-core porn."

"I signed a release. They can show my image anywhere," a punk girl said, and started crying. "I was just in a scene where I was pulled towards this girl and told to make out. They didn't say what they wanted me to do until they started shooting. I felt pressured to do it."

"I don't know if I want to do this anymore," said a woman near me. "I think I might go home."

"How?" demanded another woman. "We're in the middle of nowhere. Do *you* know where the closest subway stop is?" Most of us shook our heads.

Just then the production supervisor, a short woman with headgear attached to her walkie-talkie, pushed her way into the tent and called my name and three others. We were led to a room and left there. I was trying to figure out how I felt about the whole setup. Unlike a lot of the others, I had no problem kissing girls. But I felt bad for the straight women: They'd never kissed girls before, and now they looked traumatized, being made to do it for the first time with total strangers, in front of all these guys. Besides, did I want to be part of a bunch of straight white boys' sick lesbo fantasy?

Though I still felt some of the thrill of being in a real live music video, it was fading fast.

When a production person came in, I asked, "Am I expected to pull my pants down for this scene?" He nodded. "Then I'm out of here," I said, making up my mind. "Who do I talk to?"

"The production supervisor," he said.

I went back to the tent and spoke with the other girls who were also feeling uncomfortable. Dozens of us decided to voice our complaints to the supervisor as one united front.

First she tried to convince us we were turning down the chance to be Art. "The director is brilliant," she said. "This video is his vision of the world's chaos culminating in a lesbian group-sex scene."

Great, I thought. *Lesbian sex is part of the world's chaos?*

"If you walk off, you're not getting paid," the supervisor insisted.

I was livid and reaching my boiling point: *Some of the girls are crying. This is enough already!*

Together, as a group, we argued with the supervisor: "You brought us to the middle of nowhere and then pressured us to perform sexual acts that were *not* in the job description. We've been here since 11:00 A.M." It was now 2:00 or 3:00 in the morning. "You are going to pay us."

In the end, with fifty women crowding around her and demanding to be paid, the supervisor gave in. She paid us and arranged a van to take us home. By the time we were dropped off in Manhattan, we all felt as if we'd known each other for years. As the van pulled away, we broke into a group scream, howling out our frustration and triumph in the cold city night.

sabrina margarita alcantara-tan (bamboogirl@aol.com) is an adventurous New York gal and editrix of *Bamboo Girl* zine (www.bamboogirl.com), a publication hell-bent on empowering young women of color, especially those of Asian descent.

∞

Spreading My Legs for Womankind
molly kenefick

Ever wonder how doctors learn to do pelvic exams? Well, I can answer that question for more than six hundred medical students: I taught them—on my body.

At some medical schools, students learn to do the exam on cadavers, women under anesthesia, or with "pelvic models" (women who function simply as bodies for professors to demonstrate on). Students on the campuses where I teach learn from "pelvic educators," women who instruct students in anatomy, physiology, palpation techniques, and various emotional and cultural issues that arise in a clinical setting.

When I first heard about the job, it sounded amazing. I'd already been working to overcome negative feelings about my body (the same body-image crap most women internalize growing up in our culture), and this seemed like a good next step. More important, I felt that teaching future doctors to do sensitive, thorough pelvic exams could positively impact the lives of many female patients down the line. I thought of Joan Rivers's joke that there should be a commemorative stamp of a woman on an examining table, feet in the footrests, to honor those who keep their annual appointments. I remember thinking at the time, *Joan is right: Many women do dread the exam. But it shouldn't have to be horrible.* Now, years later, I take pride in teaching my students the many details that can make an exam a positive, comforting experience.

I was scared at first. I'd take the hospital gown into the bathroom to change, and then climb onto the table, holding the johnny tight to make sure nothing extra was exposed. I felt shy about opening my legs to strangers (especially without any foreplay!), so as I did this, I avoided looking students in the eyes. I steeled myself by acting nonchalant and businesslike, and held onto the idea that this was important to women. Now, after six years, I simply turn my back to change (yes, in front of students), wrap a sheet around me, and casually hop onto the table.

Working with two to four students at a time, I first go over psychosocial issues. I tell them that though their patient may be an adult, it could be her first exam. I suggest they offer her a hand mirror so she can see what they are doing, and that they explain what they're doing as they do it. We discuss asking questions without making assumptions about a patient's sexual orientation or practices; looking for signs of sexual abuse, and, if they suspect it, how to handle it; words patients use to describe their anatomy; and culturally specific sexual customs.

Then it's time for the physical exam. I undress from the waist down and sit on the exam table, feet in the footrests ("Not stirrups; it's not a saddle"). I teach draping technique ("Expose only the area you will be examining"), the physician's first touch ("Put your hands by the outside of her knees, and ask her to bring her knees to meet your hands—that way *she* touches *you* first"), and subsequent touch techniques ("Clinical touch should feel as different from sexual touch as possible"). We start with the external exam, checking beneath the pubic hair for redness, lice, and scabies ("Don't mention lice and scabies unless she has them"). The external exam includes inspecting the vulva, perineum, and anus ("Always avoid touching the clitoris").

The internal exam is next. I teach them to insert an index finger to find my cervix and check my glands for infection and my vaginal walls for laxity. I demonstrate how to put in and open the speculum ("Warm it first, for patient comfort"). Then we view the cervix (a first sighting and a thrill for most students) and practice the Pap smear.

Next, the bimanual exam. With two fingers inside me, a student checks for cervical tenderness and feels for the uterus. The outside hand palpates the abdomen, pushing down toward the inside fingers. The most rewarding part for students is finding an ovary (yet another first), which feels like an almond hidden under layers of pastry dough ("The number of layers depends on how much pastry I've eaten"). Lastly, a student inserts one finger in my rectum, another in my vagina. They are often surprised at how much better they can feel my uterus from two angles.

In separate sessions with students, I also teach breast exams. The first time I did this, I looked at my 38-C breasts (heavy and pendulous: nipples soft, not pert) and wished they were perkier. Then I thought, *Who the hell looks like a centerfold in real life?* I'm a real woman, and this is what women look like. More important, this is what their patients will look like. My self pep talk ended with: *You're healthy. Get over it. Focus on the work.*

With up to eight students, we first practice on a silicone-filled model (with quite lumpy breasts). I show them the palpation technique: Fingers make circles of light, medium, and deep pressure as they move in a vertical stripe pattern (lawnmower versus zigzag). Then I take off my shirt and bra and we look for rashes, dimpling, and changes in the nipples (such as spontaneous discharge or inversion). I teach them to palpate my nodes along the clavicle and under the armpit ("No tickling!"). Then, one at a time, they practice the vertical stripe technique on my breast.

Most students have been a pleasure to teach. A few had terrible palpation skills (I can only hope they've gone into research). Two got noticeable erections (I sympathized, as they seemed mortified at this betrayal of their body). A couple were inappropriate (one kept asking if my parents and boyfriend knew I did this work), and one asked me out (though I thought, *Wouldn't this be a story to tell our grandkids?* I said *no,* of course). The majority of my students, however, have been respectful and grateful for the opportunity to learn from, and on, me.

I'm amazed by all the ways this job has impacted my life. As hoped (and as strange as it may sound), undressing in front of strangers has made me more comfortable with my body. Now, years into the job, I take off my shirt and bra, drop my pants, and often feel like a superhero. I'm not a "perfect 10," just a healthy, strong woman, unashamed of her body. I feel students' admiration and respect, and I deserve it because I am doing important work for women and women's health. In addition, I've become knowledgeable about my reproductive health. Knowing where my uterus is and what my cervix looks like makes me more in touch with being a woman. On the downside, as "party talk" goes, telling people I'm a pelvic educator can be a conversation starter—or stopper. And at times, no amount of kisses could summon my libido because it got lost earlier in the day during the third pelvic exam. In general, however, I've found this to be rewarding work, both because of the immediate positive changes I see in my students and because of the ripple effect I know my work will have on their future patients. Finally, a nice benefit is that every day when I go to work, I'm reminded that *Hey, I've got ovaries.*

molly kenefick (mollykenefick@yahoo.com), a recovering "good Catholic girl," founded PassionPress.com, an erotic audio publishing company in the San Francisco Bay area that emphasizes and celebrates women's pleasure. Molly lives in Oakland, California.

CHAPTER 4

Danger: Risking Life or Limb

ADVENTURESOME

WALKING ON THE RAZOR'S EDGE

death defying

The women and girls in this chapter are risking their lives. Or at least a trip to the hospital.

When we read their stories we might think, *I could never do that!* But they might have thought that, too. Before. So then is there a potential daredevil in each of us? If so, what has to happen inside a girl's head to make her decide to put herself in harm's way? What has to happen in a woman's heart to move her to risk her life?

These women are motivated. They are inspired by needs that take a variety of forms: an instinct for survival, a lust for adventure, an impulse toward self-defense, a calling to help another, a dream that must be pursued. The potential hazards just don't matter. Meeting those needs takes precedence over everything else—worries, fear, even safety.

Some of the women here actually enjoy danger! They purposefully incorporate adrenalizing activities into their lives with the work they do, where they live, or how they play (read: *Xtreme sports*).

Pretty remarkable, considering that the message girls have gotten for eons is to be cautious, certainly not to *put* themselves in the line of fire. And if women somehow found themselves in that line, they were to wait for some benevolent Y chromosome—Prince Charming, James Bond, Batman?—to save them. The message was clear: Women were not to participate in their own rescuing.

Well, here, the damsels in distress do. In fact, the reality is that gutsy broads have been taking an active, primary role in their own saving since women have walked the Earth.

These stories illustrate what women are truly capable of, and some of the many ways their risk-taking can be expressed. Some planned, some not; some wise, some foolhardy; some about fun, others about survival—these acts show that women and girls can be aggressive and engage in life-threatening, taking-it-right-to-the-edge-of-the-cliff behavior that traditionally they've been told they'd better leave for others.

Adventures in the Jungle

denise grant

The summer before my senior year in high school, I worked as a cashier at a movie theater near an area of Los Angeles nick-named the Jungle. In the late 1980s, the Jungle was an econom-ically and socially depressed district. Many of its inhabitants were angry, unemployed, disillusioned, or on drugs. This movie theater was one of the few money-generating businesses in the area. In many ways it was a cool, air-conditioned oasis in a land of heated despair. Because of the gang-infested location of the theater, we had unusual rules and regulations for admittance, including "No hats or headwear for men." Hat colors and styles were one of the ways a local could show his gang affiliation.

I liked my job at the theater, as did most of the people who worked there. With our first-run movies, freshly popped pop-corn, and a guaranteed secure environment, everyone felt we were in some small way giving something positive to the com-munity.

One unusually hot day, a questionable looking gentleman came to the front desk to purchase a ticket for himself and his two young sons.

"I can sell you tickets," I said, as I casually flipped through the latest *Glamour,* "but I can't let you in until you remove the rollers and scarf."

I was certain that his bright blue hair curlers and navy blue bandanna indicated gang affiliation. And although there was a sign clearly stating the rules of admission above the theater's entrance, this guy became absolutely furious at me. He stood at the cashier's booth (with his boys standing behind him), screaming and berating me for almost ten minutes. Everyone in the theater lobby—children, elders, my coworkers—could hear his yelling and cursing. I stood there eyes wide, head tilted, and mouth agape, alternating between shock and embarrassment, for me and for this guy standing before me in blue rollers. Eventually, my boss came over to reason with the irate customer. It didn't work. Security was summoned to escort him off the premises.

Not more than thirty minutes later, I was in line at a local fast-food fried chicken place with some friends from work. I was complaining about my horrible encounter with the guy at the theater, when who should burst through the door but the same guy and his two sons. I hadn't expected him, but I wasn't at all surprised to see him either. He began cursing and calling me all sorts of names again—and then he pulled out a huge, steel-gray gun. (I later learned it was a 9mm.) Wild-eyed and sweaty, with his sons in tow, he walked toward me screaming, "Now how tough are you, now that you're not behind that glass? I could kill you right now!"

Yes, he could. But for some reason I remained calm, observing the entire incident with a detached sense of amusement: It all seemed so unreal—a gangbanger, a gun, my life on the line? The restaurant patrons stared at the two of us, likely wishing they had been in the mood for burgers and not chicken that day.

At the time, I was seventeen years old, five feet tall, weighing in at less than a hundred pounds, and possessing more mouth than brains. Anyway, something inside me snapped. This man had cursed and berated me at the theater for what seemed like an eternity and now had the gall to follow me here on my lunch break . . . *and pull out a gun?*

I don't think so.

I stepped away from my friends and toward the guy: "If it will make you feel like a big man in front of your two kids to shoot a ninety-pound teenager, then just go ahead and shoot." My anger fueling me, I started to walk even closer to him, "Just shoot me. What's wrong? I'm not behind the counter now."

From the corner of my eye, I could see the people in the restaurant literally drop their chicken wings, corn on the cob, and biscuits, and witness this insane scene. My two friends were behind me, in complete shock, as they later told me. The guy must have been surprised, too. For a moment he just froze, staring at me.

"What are you waiting for?" I screamed, becoming hysterical and lunging toward him. "I thought you were going to kill me!" I was enraged. *Just who did he think he was anyway?*

He hadn't counted on my being as crazy as he was. Frankly, neither had I. He started backing away, slowly at first, then turned around and ran, yelling *"Crazy bitch"* over his shoulder. His children trotted after him.

I stood there for a moment to regain my composure. A detached feeling of serenity came over me, yet at the same time I felt vindicated at having taken on the bully and won. I glanced at my Hello Kitty watch and turned to my friends, "Are you still hungry? We only have fifteen minutes left for lunch."

Sensing that the guy would not be coming back, the restaurant patrons gave me a round of applause and the managers offered me a free meal, but none of us was hungry anymore.

When we got back to the theater, my boss called the police, who questioned me about the entire drama. I didn't remember much, so my friends supplied most of the details. When I casually mentioned the incident to my parents at dinner, they wanted me to quit, saying that working in the Jungle was far too dangerous. I told them it wasn't that bad, and I wanted to finish the summer with my friends. I did, and the incident was forgotten (except by my parents) within a few days.

denise grant (sixdegrees99@hotmail.com) writes, travels, and plans events. She doesn't mind being called a "crazy bitch" if the definition of the term is someone who always fights for the underdog—including when it is herself.

∞

Slapshot off the Rink
amy chambers

Everyone who knows me knows I'm a big hockey fan, so it wasn't surprising that I was at my boyfriend's game. During the event, I watched with the rest of the crowd as the two teams were violent on the ice. We all figured it would cool off after the game ended.

Wrong.

On the trip back to the locker room, one of the other team's players started trash-mouthing one of ours. A fight broke out between the two, and soon everyone from both teams was involved. Before I knew what I was doing, *I jumped in to break up the fight.* First, I grabbed a player from our team and peeled him off some defeated doormat under him. Then I shoved aside dumbfounded bystanders.

It was exhilarating . . . a complete rush. It was like my whole being had abandoned my body and was now watching myself break up this jumble of brawling bodies. Sure, I was scared being in the thick of it. I could practically *feel* the fear pulsing through my veins. But that didn't stop me, because I was also ticked off. I suppose that's why I started screaming at *all* the players—as if they didn't each outweigh me by a whopping one hundred pounds! When the players and I came to our senses, the fight ended with the exchange of a few vulgar words and the referees escorting everyone (except me) to their respective locker rooms.

Driving home, I realized what a crazy person I was. I thanked God for being a woman—if I was a guy, I could've gotten my butt seriously kicked. Maybe next time I'll offer to be a target for the pig pile at a football game.

amy chambers (BigCat20@discoverymail.com) is a college girl who doesn't usually get into brawls. No, usually she volunteers as an emergency medical technician with the Tri-Town Terrorcats high-school hockey team.

∞

Not Minding My Own Business
mary ann mccourt

Two years ago, as I was driving down a major street on my way home from work, I passed a young man hitting a teenage girl and throwing her to the ground. As I zipped by, I saw her repeatedly get up and try to run, only to have the guy push her down again and again. Now past them, I looked in my rearview mirror and saw him dragging her into the bushes. *My god, he's going to rape her.* Almost without thinking, I made an illegal U-turn on the busy road and pulled up alongside where he was slapping and dragging her.

"Leave her alone!" I shouted, as I jumped out of my car. Part of me couldn't believe I was getting in the middle of this, but mostly I was too enraged at this guy to stop myself.

The girl stood up again, and ran toward me with a look of sheer panic on her face.

"Get in the car," I yelled to her. That was all I could say at the time: "Get in the car," I repeated, though by now she was almost inside.

Before I could breathe a sigh of relief, her assailant followed after her, and the realization suddenly struck me, *Ohmygod, what if he has a knife or a gun? I have two young kids at home, what would they do without me?* I didn't even have a car phone to call for help. So I shouted at him again, "You! You stay right where you are. The police are on their way." A big fat lie.

"Whaddya mean?" he said.

"You heard me, I called the police. Stay away from her."

Meanwhile, people were driving by in their cars. I looked at the faces of the drivers as they sped past, hoping someone might stop and offer help. Instead, they gawked and drove on. I couldn't help thinking, *What if I had acted like all those other apathetic drivers? Who knows what he would have done to her?*

As the teenager climbed into my car, her attacker began pleading: "Don't do it, baby, don't go with that lady." Luckily, she closed the door fast and we sped away.

Now where should we go? I wondered. *Of course.* "I want to take you to the police station, to fill out a report," I said.

The girl was breathing hard, catching her breath, and visibly shaken. "I don't know . . . maybe I should just go back to class . . . can you drop me off at the high school?"

"High school?" I asked. So young. "Is that guy your boyfriend?"

Turns out they had been dating for three years, since she was just fourteen. Now she was seventeen, and he was in his twenties. This was not the first occurrence of violent behavior. It was ongoing and getting worse—including the night before, when he had smashed the windshield of her family's car. I could tell just by looking at her that she was deathly afraid of him. I'd seen the look before: My sister's boyfriend had stalked her. I tried to convince the girl that she needed to get some help, today.

When we arrived at the station, we both wrote down our versions of the story. But she obviously didn't want to go through with any procedures. Fortunately, she did call her parents. The officer said the police department would contact me to testify if she decided to press charges. Behind the girl's back, the officer added, "Don't hold your breath."

Before I left this young girl I was now so afraid for, I told her how hard we'd worked to keep my younger sister out of danger. It was not easy, but in the end, my sister's ex-boyfriend stopped bothering her. As I pulled the keys out of my purse, I said, "I'm scared if you stay with this guy, I'll be reading about you in the death notices." I had never felt so sure of anything in my life.

She looked at me with tears in her eyes. "You're not the only one who thinks that."

This story doesn't have a happy ending; it has a real-life ending. I was never called to testify. I don't know what happened to this poor girl. I pray she is safe and happy, but deep down I know she is just one of many women and girls who, for any number of complex and personal reasons, stay in abusive and sometimes deadly relationships.

In a way, I can't believe what I did that afternoon, especially given how crazy and violent people can be these days. But I'm sure I'd do it again if I saw the same thing happening tomorrow.

Wouldn't you?

mary ann mccourt (McCourtsky@aol.com), today a mother of three, cares about all young people. She works in the Metro Detroit area for the Infant Mortality Project, a nonprofit organization dedicated to reducing infant deaths. She now owns a car phone, for emergencies such as these.

∞

Surfergrrl

elaine marshall

Learning to skydive is electrifying. At two miles up (as in *in the sky*), I smiled crazily at my instructor, a strapping Vietnam vet I called *Mommy,* let go of the airplane, and slipped into the utter freedom and excitement of falling through the air at more than 150 miles per hour.

As I lay panting and pale-faced on the ground after my first jump, a seasoned sky diver who had heard my screams during free fall kneeled down beside me. "Congratulations," he said. "You just experienced your first airgasm." The sport of skydiving had initiated its newest adrenaline junkie; knees shaking, ears pounding, clothes damp with sweat, I hobbled to the ticket window to sign up for a second jump.

Skydiving is never boring. Sometimes it is downright terrifying. But the initial shocks of adrenaline I experienced as a student soon gave way to the calmer pleasure of enjoying bird's-eye views and mastering the art of flying my own body. So with 550 jumps under my belt, I decided to give *skysurfing* a try.

Skysurfing has pushed the boundaries of skydiving, a sport in which risks are carefully calculated (honest). The pro who flies a fifty-five-inch surfing board through a series of freestyle spins, flips, and twists is regarded by some skydivers as a renegade, a lunatic. Sounded like my kind of sport! The prospect of leaping from an airplane with my feet strapped together on a stiff metal board brought back that familiar feeling of dread, which, I realized somewhat sickeningly, I welcomed. I called to schedule my first lesson.

On a chilly Saturday morning, I met with Mike, a tall, athletic skysurfing pioneer who would teach me what little there was to know about this new sport that involved swooshing through the sky on an air-designed snowboard. Mike showed me how to strap into a puny-looking, twenty-four-inch beginner's skyboard and accustom myself to the "trauma," as he insisted on calling it, of having my feet restricted to an object that exerted its own forces in free fall. Should I find myself trapped and spinning uncontrollably under the skyboard, as skysurfers sometimes do, I had merely to yank on an emergency release that would send the board to Earth under its own mini-parachute.

After practicing on the ground and taking a few warm-up skydives, Mike concluded his coaching with a warning: "Skysurfing is a dangerous and demanding exercise in dexterity. Spins can get extremely violent. I know a guy who lost control and was unable to release the board from one of his feet. He started spinning around helplessly and says he doesn't even remember pulling [i.e., opening his canopy]. He landed with his eyes full of blood and a face covered with purple dots. Had he gone much longer, he probably would have suffered a stroke from the G forces."

Gulp.

Now two miles up, feet bound to the board, I braced my arms inside the doorway of the airplane and leaned my body out against the cold, rough blast of air. I stared vacantly at the square plots of farmland below and the enormous blue sky around me, took a deep breath, and vaulted free to ride a 45-degree slope out the door. I held a downhill snowboard position for almost two seconds before the board unexpectedly pulled my body into a series of washing-machine twists and turns. As I fought furiously to regain control, Mike's words about *trauma* drifted through my spinning head. A burst of adrenaline surged through my body, and I forced myself on top of the board. That's when the ride got fun. My speed doubled and I darted through the sky, ears numb with the roar of the wind, face pulled back by the velocity, and eyes watering beneath my loosening goggles.

Looking at my altimeter, I saw I was dangerously low. I instantly fell into the flat, free-fall position necessary for pulling. Unfortunately, this move forced the board above me. It acted like a demon rudder and I began vacillating and pitching roughly, too unstable to pull safely. Another bolt of energy shot through my bloodstream, and I was able to stabilize my body for a fraction of a second. I pulled. After my canopy popped open, I hung there, floating to Earth, wild-eyed and gasping.

Just before landing, I released the bindings and kicked the board free (turfsurfing in is reserved for the experts). Endorphins swamped my brain as I touched ground. Already Mike's earnest warnings to progress slowly were fading as a louder, more insistent voice screamed, "I WANT A BIGGER BOARD! I WANT A BIGGER BOARD!"

My second jump was more fun. After gaining the stand-up position, I leaned forward over the board, kept my back straight, and felt the sensations of lift and glide—of *surfing*. I did a few turns and generally just played with my new toy. Next I graduated to my "BIGGER BOARD." The wider, thirty-inch model was harder to control, but that meant a bigger endorphin rush and a more exhilarating experience of riding the sky.

Learning to skysurf reminded me of learning to skydive. Both are about performing in spite of choking fear. Both give me the feeling of mastering my own body and busting past boundaries others respect without question. I enjoy looking around at the skydivers and surfers on the drop zone packing their parachutes, carrying their boards, and swapping stories. We come back weekend after weekend, forever infatuated with the charge that comes when we squeeze all the sweet juice we can muster out of life. To risk my life, after all, is not nearly as dangerous as to risk never really living.

elaine marshall (itchyink@hotmail.com), a writer living in Switzerland, had trouble deciding which of her bazillion gutsy stories she should submit. Squatting with anarchists in England? Spending a winter in a Yosemite cave? Sleeping alone in cemeteries? In the end, the potential of "eyes full of blood and a face covered with purple dots" won.

War Zone
anonymous

We were huddled together in a grass hut lit by candlelight, waiting for the guerilla fighters' word that the timing was right for our crossing of the lagoon. It was midnight and we had traveled since early morning to reach the southernmost tip of this war-torn country. In the United States, with its high-speed highways, it would have taken us three hours. Instead, in humid, hundred-degree heat, we crammed into a van without air-conditioning and endured road conditions that challenged even the most skilled jungle drivers for twenty-one endless hours.

My colleague and I were associates of a university-based conflict resolution program. We were making this grueling trek to the south of the country with two guides and a journalist in hopes that we would be granted a meeting with the leadership of a sophisticated and disciplined liberation movement. The rebels had been fighting for independence from the ruling government for more than a decade, in a war that had taken tens of thousands of lives. We decided that though a meeting was not guaranteed, we would make the trip to show the guerillas we were sincere in our desire to understand the conflict from their point of view. Understanding each side's perspective is the third party's first step in any conflict resolution process. We hoped this course might eventually lead to a face-to-face meeting between the warring parties.

The logistical arrangements of our trip were in the hands of Catholic priests trusted by both sides. Fortunately, they didn't tell us about the potential dangers we would face. We were nervous enough; after all, this was the heart of a violent, protracted ethnic conflict. Anything could happen. We could be caught by government forces, perhaps, or caught in the cross fire of a skirmish. We chose not to think about it.

We were told that with government forces patrolling the lagoon, we'd have a better chance of escaping their scrutiny if we crossed in the dark of night, when rebel boats turned off their navigation lights and maneuvered by starlight alone—everyone wanted to avoid flagging the government's attention. Anxiously waiting in the hut, we drank tea served by our rebel hosts and engaged in conversation with our priest guides, one of whom was an amateur astronomer. Perhaps he decided to give us a lecture on astronomy to distract us from our nervousness. Leading us outside, directing our gaze to the magnificent constellations filling the sky, he convinced us that our view would be even more splendid from the boat. This made us almost excited about making what we knew would be a risky and illegal crossing.

At 2:00 A.M., the rebels determined we should begin our hour-and-a-half trip. We walked to the water's edge to a rowboat with a small outboard engine on the back. *This couldn't be for all five of us?* I thought. It was. Fear for our physical safety rose up my chest and into my throat. Two young guerilla fighters, no more than sixteen years old, were to take us across. I looked them over, hoping to find reassurance that it was okay to put my life in their hands. It did not take long to conclude that these boys, who had given up so much to fight for national independence, were not only competent but filled with a determination and purpose the likes of which I had rarely seen. Witnessing the young men's strength, I decided to override my initial emotional response: I swallowed my fear and stepped into the overfull, rocking boat.

All was going well until halfway through our journey. In the middle of the lagoon, the motor spurted fumes and then stopped. Suddenly we became stationary and dangerously perfect targets, undetectable to other unlit boats whizzing past. A bolt of panic shot through me as I envisioned being hit, boat splintering to bits, bodies lost in the dark waters below.

To calm us, the priest began his second astronomy lecture, but I was unable to concentrate on his words. I studied the young guerillas' every move as they repeatedly lifted the engine out of the water in an attempt to locate the problem. It was a combination of physical and mental inventiveness and ingenuity that left me awestruck. I may have felt scared, but I never doubted I was in good hands. I was seeing a small example of what the liberation movement was capable of—endurance in the face of great odds. A part of me relaxed, and I was able to tune into the lecture on celestial masterpieces.

After what became a tense hourlong wait, the guerillas finally restarted the engine, and in another hour we saw the shoreline. Due to our delay, by the time we neared land, the tide had receded and the boat was unable to navigate any closer to the beach. We would have to walk a mile through the water, waist-deep, to reach the shore. I looked at my colleagues, exchanging glances of sheer panic. *Could we possibly walk that far in the water in the dead of night, our belongings over our heads, not knowing what we were stepping on, with only the stars to guide us?* I was sure I had used up all my reserves of courage just making it across the lagoon. So where was I to reach to find the strength to fight my fears that were now winning me over?

I did not have time to think about it. We were hastily ushered off the boat and into the water before I knew it. I looked at the journalist accompanying us, our eyes locked for a second, and she said, "Just keep walking." With every breathless step I took, I realized that this was a war zone, and for once in my life, instead of reading about it, I was part of it.

Regardless of my utter exhaustion and a mind full of worries, by 4:00 A.M. we reached the beach. We were quickly taken to a convent and greeted by a nun, her face lit only by the candle she was holding. (The city, immersed in war, was virtually without electricity.) I took one look at the nun and wanted to run into her arms and cry. I knew she was aware of what we had been through, her face communicating more than just her warm welcome. For years she had been working with the local people, living in the midst of this deadly conflict. We followed her quiet steps to a bedroom, where she urged us to sleep.

Two days after our arrival, we were granted a meeting with the rebel leadership. We were grateful for the opportunity to hear their perspective on the conflict and to introduce ourselves and our work. Our experience in the country, however, was much more than that two-hour meeting. The tenacity and fearlessness I had witnessed in the people—our guides, the young rebels in the boat, the nun—and the inspiring way they conducted their lives in the face of constant danger, helped me to see that the distinction between what we think we cannot do and what we must do is often not a matter of choice. On a personal level, I was brought face-to-face with my own fears, which I discovered were more relenting than I had thought. Experiencing fear can paradoxically move us more toward courage than cowardice.

the author travels around the globe to facilitate meetings between the leaders of conflicting, and often warring, ethnic groups. She figures you'll understand why she had to obfuscate a few specific facts in this story, such as locations, numbers, and her name.

∞

Impossible Choices: From El Salvador to the United States
eva

In late 1993, I left my home, my town, my country, my children—my six children. I thought only of them when I made the decision—and it tore at my heart.

I was the only parent they had. Their father, my husband, had left years earlier when I was pregnant with our youngest, making our economic situation very difficult. My minimum-wage salary as a secretary wasn't enough. It paid for three days of food and four days of worry. I faced a hard choice: Remain in El Salvador, unable to provide the clothes and food my kids needed, and the education they deserved, or get to the United States where I could work and send money home so they could have a decent life—but without a mother. When my parents offered to care for them, my father was insistent: "What's going to happen to you here with six kids, alone? You *have* to go to help your children."

My sister, who had already made the hazardous trip to the United States, sent a letter:

Querida Eva,

   You must understand the dangers. Along the way, not only are there robbers who will kill you for your money or simply the clothes you are wearing, but also *people get lost*. Some are purposefully abandoned, left by the coyotes.

She said the coyotes, guides for those making the illegal border crossing, take ten, fifteen, thirty people, demanding half the money ($2,500 per person) in advance. Yet if they decide they don't have enough to cover the costs of the whole group, they purposely "lose" a few en route and proceed on.

I knew it was a chance I had to take for my children. My generous sister sent the $2,500, so I gathered my strength and put my faith in God. I left home while my youngest slept. The older ones, fourteen, twelve, and ten, were crying and hugging me good-bye as I left in the dark of early morning. I brought nothing with me, just my pants and blouse, my sadness and tears.

We walked for endless days through El Salvador and Guatemala, passing lush, green mountains. I barely noticed their beauty due to my grief and my anxiety about the uncertainties ahead. Our four coyotes quickly became abusive, hitting us and threatening further violence. One night they raped the fourteen-year-old girl from our group, in front of all of us. She was sobbing and screaming, we all were, but we couldn't stop them. Our lives, and those of our children back home, depended on our enduring their abuse. We spent two weeks with these men.

In Mexico, with new coyotes, things got worse. Fear became our daily companion. We walked through the jungle for days at a time, scanning the bushes for robbers, coyotes (real ones), cobras, and dangerous *pantanos*—quicksand-like swamps. We were soaked much of the time from crossing river after river, sometimes at night, illegally. When some were too scared to cross in unsafe and rickety rafts, the coyotes dismissed them, saying, "Then stay." Once our group got lost in the thick of the jungle for a full day. We walked without food, unable to find a path out. When we made it to a river at nightfall, we were so hungry we caught crawfish and ate them raw. Occasionally, we paid men to drive us in perilously overcrowded cars. Once we spent four days straight on a train with nothing to eat but peanuts.

Wherever I was, whatever I was doing, constant worries chased me: How are my children doing without me? Will they be okay? What if I am killed? My family does not know where I am or how I am doing. They won't know what happened to me. I am alone.

Our coyotes in Mexico hit the women, grabbed them, and sometimes took one away, out of sight for a while. One night they threatened to throw each of us into the river and drown us unless we did what they wanted. What they wanted was to rape all the women of our group at once.

I was trembling, terrified, as I approached one of the coyotes, a man from my hometown. Half begging, half threatening, I said, "Please, if you let them rape me, I'll escape and tell both of our families back home." He knew that meant they would all openly condemn him.

He spoke with the other coyotes, then said, "Don't worry, they won't do anything to you. But you aren't to leave this room, or even open the door."

"What about the other women?"

"I can't do anything about that. Just take care of yourself. The others aren't important."

That night, I heard screaming, sobbing, hitting, and blows. Asking for God's help, I sat huddled alone in that room, crying all night long.

The following day, and for days after, all the women were still in tears. The men had even raped the fourteen-year-old again. We went numb; we had already paid our money, a huge sum, and on some level felt it no longer mattered what happened to us because we were going to be living in the United States, and that was enough.

In Mexicali, on New Year's Eve, we attempted to cross the border by scurrying through dark, dirty, underground storm drains with only flashlights to light the way. The Border Patrol caught some of us, including a señora and me. It was a nightmare. The prison guards hit us to get—they said—the truth: our names, where we were from, why we had come. We lied, saying we were Mexicans, so that when they returned us "home" we wouldn't have to start from El Salvador again. The whole two hours in prison, the señora and I couldn't stop crying.

After they "returned" us to Mexico, we waited three days and, determined, tried again, this time from Tijuana. We watched the Border Patrol, and when we saw them arresting other people trying to cross, that was when we ran and ran. I was shaking with fear all the way, but we made it!

It had been six weeks of terror and tears. Like the others, I was traumatized. After making it to the United States, I tried to forget the hell we had all lived through. What else could I do? I found work quickly in a fruit-packing factory and sent money to my children as soon as possible.

I am comfortable here with my sister in the United States, though I never stop feeling the lump of sadness sitting in my stomach and throat—my children are so far away. If you asked me today if I made the right decision by coming, I can't say I did. My kids need me, and instead they have to grow up without me. My littlest, only two when I left, doesn't even know me. At least they have money to live on, are in school, and have a future. Before, I could not say that. I don't feel it was the *right* choice to come to the United States, but I don't feel there *was* a right choice—either way, my kids suffered.

Last month, seven years after my trip, my twenty-one-year-old daughter arrived. I was worried about her making the journey, but she knew the dangers and insisted on coming. Luckily she didn't face any problems, and though the ache I feel from missing my other children has not gone away, at least now my daughter and I have each other.

eva, who chooses not to use her full name, urges all women of the world to think carefully before leaving their children. (Eva told this story to Rivka in Spanish and together they translated and wrote the final draft. Rivka is incredibly impressed with Eva's strength, courage, and commitment to her children.)

∞

Documenting It
ruchira gupta

As we were about to enter the doorway of the brothel, my cameraman suddenly turned to me. "It's too dangerous. I'm not going to do it. I'm not filming any more. My equipment is expensive; it could get damaged. We could get *killed!"*

He had a point. The fourteen-block red-light district we were in was no picnic. It was controlled by ruthless gangs, protected by India's senior-ranking politicians, and patrolled by corrupt, paid-off cops. There was a powerful nexus between these groups and the mafia, which ran the country's sex trade. Danger was all around. As we investigated our story, we were constantly told in polite and not-so-polite ways, "Don't do this!" Cops harassed us, intelligence agencies stalked us, and everywhere we parked, mafia goons stoned our car. We ventured into the lawless brothels without any protection from anyone. Once we climbed their narrow stairways, there was no easy escape; we were at the mercy of the often violent thugs inside. We had to make a decision to do it and not think about the consequences. But now, a few days into the filming, at the doorway of a particularly menacing-looking brothel, my hefty, six-foot-tall camera-man got spooked.

I was, too, but my outrage at the exploitation I had seen, and my need to do something about it, pushed me forward. I was going into the brothels so I could expose the horrors inside—the hundreds of thousands of girl sex slaves imprisoned in Bombay, India.

I looked up at my cameraman, "If I, who am half your size, can do it—*and can even go in ahead of you*—why can't you? I face worse consequences: I could be raped, too." I guess I shamed him sufficiently, because as I headed up the rat-infested stairs, he followed me.

It had been a year earlier when I had visited Nepal and stumbled upon village after village void of girls.

"Where are all the girls?" I asked everyone.

"In Bombay." A snicker or a slimy look usually accompanied the answer. "Don't you know that the girls go off for prostitution?"

I didn't. *"All of them?"*

I came to learn that the sale of girls is no secret; it is all done in the open, like any business. There is the local procurer, an uncle or fellow villager, who buys the girl from her parents for twenty to thirty dollars. He'll collect three or four females, aged seven to thirty, bring them to a bigger town, collect another dozen girls from other rural areas, put them all in a truck, smuggle them over the Nepal-India border (where he'll pay off the border police), then sell them to the next middleman up the chain, in India. The new men take the girls to small boarding-houses. There they rape the girls, beat them, subjugate their spirits completely until they do whatever these men want. The men sometimes use ice to break in the premenstrual girls. Then the girls are taken to Bombay and sold to brothel madams for three thousand rupees apiece, about forty to fifty dollars.

Back in Bombay, I heard how the half-grown children are bonded sex slaves for the first five years, unpaid and forced to "service" twenty-five to thirty men a day: *raped* twenty-five to thirty times a day! "Clients" stub out cigarettes on their young breasts and shove bottles up their vaginas. They are kept in five-by-seven-foot rooms, each crammed with about four miniature beds. The rooms have no walking space, just beds and curtains separating them. Windows are barred, entrances locked and guarded. A severe beating follows any attempt to flee. After five years, they are allowed to keep half their meager earnings. By then the madams have made sure that the girls have become addicted to drugs and alcohol and have had a baby, so they won't run. The girls, now with distorted, almost caricatured bodies, get trapped by disease and debt—they have to pay for water, bedding, and food. By age forty they are usually dead from AIDS.

I learned that this horror goes on around the globe, from Africa to Albania. Each year 4 million girls are sold by their impoverished parents, tricked with false promises of good jobs, or outright kidnapped. They are brought to big cities in their own country or sent abroad to rich Western nations. Fifty thousand are shipped to the United States each year.

It's a whole institution, I realized. *Like the arms or narcotics trade, like gold smuggling. Only this is the* flesh *trade.* I'd uncovered something, and now, risky or not, I had to investigate it. *No one should have to go through this—especially kids,* I thought. *And if I can't hold the powerful, faceless men who run the industry accountable, maybe I can make* society *realize what is going on here.* I contacted the Canadian Broadcasting Corporation. When they funded my proposed documentary and supplied me with a crew, I set out for the brothels of Bombay.

I already had two documentaries under my belt, but this would be my first focusing on women. I considered the difficulties ahead. The girls didn't trust anyone. They felt everyone was always out to get something from them. And they were right. I didn't want to participate in yet another form of their exploitation by forcing them to talk. I wanted to win their trust the real way, by earning it. So I just hung around, on the streets and in the brothels, for six months. We built friendships based on equality. We exchanged information about our lives—very intimate information. These women came to know more about me than my closest friends and family.

From day one I said, "I want to share your story with the world."

The girls didn't think anyone would be interested. "Why?" they asked skeptically. And with understandable resistance: "We don't want to tell our story." They faced discrimination, stigma all the time.

So I talked about philosophical issues with them: how women can empower each other; how women can change their own lives; how life is not simply about destiny, but also what you choose. We talked about men, too: the role of men in our lives. The role of men in *their* lives was clear.

I could tell that as they watched me interact with the men in my team (director, cameraman, sound recorders, location manager), they were discovering something—a woman friend who was also a role model they could relate to.

We were the first film crew to get inside the Bombay brothels, and we had to get permission from the madams. It was relatively easy. Instead of seeing me as a threat, they were intrigued. "We'll let you shoot if you don't film the clients," they said. We agreed.

I was inside interviewing girls almost daily for six months. I did not film the servicing of men, out of respect for the girls, but the beds next to me were usually shaking as I conducted my interviews.

This took a toll. I felt personally violated watching the violence perpetrated on these young girls. I could not be sexual or at all physical while working on the film. My grandmother, whose house I stayed in during the filming, said I often talked in my sleep: "Don't touch me!"

The emotional damage was real, but the physical risk was greater. Once, when we were in one of the tiny rooms jam-packed with small beds, we were interviewing some teenaged girls from Nepal when suddenly, abruptly, we were surrounded by men. Clients—clients closely allied with the mafia who controlled the brothel. The tension in the room became thick.

Okay, I'll just finish this interview and move out quickly, I thought. But it was too late. One man put his hand in front of the camera, another pulled out a knife and pointed it in my direction. "You're not filming," he said.

I was so immensely involved with my work, my first thought was: *But I haven't finished the interview yet!* Then my brain froze. Somehow I knew I had to get a dialogue going. "Hey, I'm not doing anything to hurt *you,*" rushed out of my mouth, and then, more cautiously: "What do you plan on doing with that knife?

"I'm not going to let you film."

"Fine, fine, we won't film. But why don't you put away the knife." Whenever there is trouble, the madams are nowhere to be found. We were alone now, with just the dangerously agitated clients and the usually passive young women.

"No. People like you should not come to the brothel," he said.

My dialogue idea was working—sort of. It seemed we had both relaxed, if only slightly. "Okay. But why don't you just let me finish what I'm doing . . ." I had a habit of pushing the envelope. Besides, I was still thinking about my incomplete interview.

Bad move. The client raised his knife to my throat and pressed. "Haven't you gotten the message? We're not going to let you continue."

My cameraman was ready to bolt—but there was no way out. One of the clients purposefully blocked the door.

I could do nothing. *We're goners,* I thought. *I hope he kills instead of just maims me.*

That is when the girls stepped in, four of them. They just moved in front of me. "No, this is our room," one said.

"*We* invited her in, and she is going to get our stories," another said.

"*You* people should leave," the first spoke up again.

The young women completely surrounded me now, getting between my body and the armed men. "You are going to have to kill us first," they declared with rare conviction.

The men shouted angrily, but then left. If it hadn't been for the girls protecting me . . . well, let's just say it was a narrow escape.

The documentary, *The Selling of Innocents,* came out a year later and won eleven international awards, including an Emmy for Outstanding Investigative Journalism. Now I show the film in rural villages as a preventative tool. In one poor village in Nepal, a father said, "I was going to let my daughter go to a brothel. At least there she'd get two meals a day. But now that I've seen the film, I'll never let her go." That single statement meant more than any award ever could.

ruchira gupta (ruchiragupta@hotmail.com) is an information and communication specialist for the United Nations Development Fund for Women (UNIFEM) (www.unifem.undp.org). After the film came out, the White House honored Ruchira for her work against sex trafficking. Her organization, Apne Aap (www.apne-aap.org), helps sex workers in Bombay's red-light district demand access to health care, obtain protection from police abuse, and curtail attacks by clients. This story was written together with Rivka after an interview.

∞

Gorilla Dreams
maite sureda

Ever since I was twelve years old, when I first learned about Jane Goodall's work with chimpanzees, I longed to follow in her footsteps: a woman, out in the wild, studying primates by herself. Unlike Goodall, though, my imagination was fired not by chimps but by gorillas. I was awed by their size, power, and grace. It never crossed my mind, however, to actually go to Africa to see and study them; it was always just a dream. My reality was my husband and two dogs here in the United States.

Then one day I saw that a university biology department was looking for a minority biologist to study birds in the Dja Wildlife Reserve in southern Cameroon, West Africa. Speechless, I read the announcement over and over. I was perfect, an Hispanic woman with all the experience they requested. But to me, the birds were a side interest. The most exciting aspect of the project was its location; that was where western lowland gorillas were found. *I have to give it a shot,* I thought, sending in my application. Within a week I heard from the project coordinator, we met, and she offered me the job on the spot. Two months later I was on a plane headed for Africa.

Before I left I brushed up on all the gorilla information I could find. As a result, I was familiar with quite a bit by the time I arrived. Once there, I asked members of the Baka tribe, who lived near the reserve, to teach me everything they knew about the gorillas native to the region. Generously, they taught me how to recognize gorilla sign, like food remains, feces, knuckle-prints, nests, and smells. Unfortunately for me, though, when the Baka sensed a gorilla close by, they would make noise to scare it away. And with good reason: Adult male gorillas, known as silverbacks, can be huge—five and a half feet tall, and up to four hundred pounds of pure muscle. They have been known to bend the steel frames of cages and rip apart a man's leg with a single bite. Running from one would be pointless. They plow through thick jungle vegetation like a bulldozer, whereas we Homo sapiens could only slowly machete our way out. By making a racket to scare away the gorillas, my guides felt they were protecting me and being respectfully cautious. I soon realized that if I wanted to see any gorillas, I would have to go into the forest alone.

Monday through Saturday I studied hornbills (my *official* reason for being at the reserve), but in the evenings I collected data on the gorilla sign that camp members and I had encountered throughout the day. Each Saturday night I planned a Sunday gorilla outing according to where the most recent sign was found. The next morning, my "day off," I'd wake at 5:00 A.M. and sit beneath a tree, listening to the incredible sound of insects in the jungle. When the sun rose, the birds started to sing and the insects quieted. That's when I'd start walking.

Four months of Sunday outings passed, and I still hadn't found any gorillas.

Then one Sunday, as I walked along the end of the K5 trail, where the dense vegetation covered the path like a tunnel, I saw very fresh gorilla sign. I walked slowly, recording everything on my notepad so I could later mark it on my "Gorilla Map." Suddenly the vegetation fifteen feet in front of me moved. I froze and slowly raised my binoculars, expecting to see a bush pig or forest antelope. Instead, a male silverback charged out of the thicket and screamed "Rrrraaa, ra, ra!" at me, then quickly dashed back into the brush.

He was all I'd hoped—beautiful, huge, and incredible.

I followed what I'd read in my gorilla books and did not run. I didn't move an inch. Not because I was frightened (though he could have killed me if he wanted to): I wasn't scared, I was in heaven and living the dream I'd had since childhood. I stayed still because I wanted the gorilla to stick around. After a couple of seconds, he did reappear, yelled another vibrant "Rrraaaaa!" then disappeared again. From the sound of it, he'd run off for good into the jungle. I tried to take notes, but I was shaking too much from the excitement. I waited for what seemed an eternity: *He might return,* I thought, hoping against hope. Yes, I knew it was dangerous to stay, but I also understood that all I had worked for, all I had hoped for since I was twelve, was finally coming true.

Before I knew it—"Rrraaa! Ra!"—another scream, from the same spot the first had been. It was the silverback again, this time behind the brush right in front of me. I was elated, and confused; I knew I'd already heard a gorilla leave. *So that had to have been* another *gorilla that fled,* I thought. I continued to wait, totally motionless, as I heard a second gorilla follow the first's lead and run off into the bush.

That's it, they're gone. The silverback, too. Oh, how lucky I am, two *gorillas in one da—*

"Rrrraaaa!" came a new cry. The silverback! He was still there, making his brilliant presence known with nonstop thunderous yells clearly directed at me. I was sure he saw me because, unlike him, I was exposed on the trail. Now I understood. There had been *three,* and it was the silverback that stayed, to protect the others in his group and defend their turf.

After five glorious minutes, in which he yelled and yelled, I finally decided I'd better leave. Slowly, I backed away, taking tiny steps. As soon as I moved, I heard the silverback move, too, in the opposite direction, screaming every few seconds to remind me he was still nearby. Once I was far enough away and felt safe, I knelt on the ground and cried like a baby. I was the happiest person on the planet. My dream had come true.

maite sureda returned from Africa to study and work with Koko, the gorilla who knows sign language. Now, as an elementary-school teacher, she works with another delightful mammal, Homo sapien children.

∞

✳ *Triumph of the Amazon Queen*
kym trippsmith

I am the Amazon Queen. I did not claim that title out of some misled Xena Warrior Princess wannabe angst. I earned the moniker after living ten years on a sixty-three-foot U.S. Navy AVR rescue boat, so named as she anchored offshore from Sausalito, California. I was an anchor-out: I lived a quarter mile from land with a two-hundred-pound weight sunk to the ocean floor to keep me from drifting away. Fed up with living as a rent slave in the city, I had bought the retired, motorless boat for five grand, got some locals to tow it out for me, and then lived for free with a million-dollar view.

The waterfront community is unique, complete with real-life pirates, Vietnam vets, hermits, drug addicts, verifiable crazies, and a few artist types (like me). This anarchistic host of misfits lives without the creature comforts the rest of society lives for. But I had other comforts very few people ever know. Every morning, seabirds played leapfrog over the waves in their quest for breakfast. Every night, the sea gently rocked me to sleep.

One particularly stormy night, I woke up to a loud crashing noise. I opened my eyes and saw a forty-five-foot fishing boat looming outside my window. It must have been dragging anchor because of the high winds, and now had karmically caught on my anchor chain. There we were, slamming into each other every thirty seconds or so with each rush of a wave. The rain came down in sheets and the wind howled like Madonna on drugs. I jumped out of bed and tried to remember my mantra—*don't panic*—as I dressed in my rain suit and scrounged around in the predawn darkness for my rain boots. In mere moments, I jumped into my little fourteen-foot wooden skiff, praying the six-horsepower Evinrude motor would start up. Luckily, it did, and I headed out into seventy-five-knot winds and five-foot, white-crested waves. I bailed water and screamed into the wind as I approached my closest neighbor.

"Hey Louie," I yelled. "You gotta come help me. Someone's fishing boat broke loose and its line is stuck on my anchor chain."

No answer.

Rain beat down like ice needles, freezing the freckles right off my face. "Louie! Wake up. I know you can hear me. I need help! It keeps slamming into the *Amazon Queen* and might just break her into tiny bite-size pieces."

A moment later he screamed back in full bravado, "Screw you. Ain't my boat. Ain't my problem."

So much for being neighborly. So much for chivalry. So much for the damn golden rule.

I zoomed off to another anchor-out's domain, ready to kill. By the time I arrived, Big Bill was already out on deck. I pulled up alongside his fifty-six-footer. I just knew he would be my salvation. I groveled a few *thank you*'s as he attached a big knife to his belt.

"Yeah, I saw you were in a little trouble there, Queenie."

Big Bill was a 280-pound pirate. Nobody crossed him. He was never one for sympathy, so I was surprised to find him ready to help. "Hey," he said, as he jumped into my skiff, "You have garlic for dinner?" Pirates aren't much for pleasantries or manners either.

With Big Bill on board, my little boat sank deeper than what I knew to be safe. Throwing caution literally to the wind, I steered against the waves as water surged in and around our tiny vessel. Blood pounded in my heart like a metronome gone crazy while I watched the two huge boats ahead of us slam into one another. Even though fear had all but taken over my entire system, I was more alive than I've ever been in my life. I felt exhilarated as we flew through the waves in spine-tingling winds.

The plan was to zoom past the intruding vessel's port side and then cut back just as we reached the stern. After that, we'd slowly approach the bow. Big Bill had one chance to reach up and cut the fishing boat's line. But then what? If he missed the line, the twenty-ton fishing boat would slam down on top of us, breaking my skiff into tiny pieces. We'd be fish food. If he cut the line, there was still a chance we'd get trapped between the two boats and smashed to bits. With death closer than it'd ever been, I summoned up the spirit of my Amazon warrior ancestors and headed toward the boat's port side.

The first part of the plan went well. I cut the 360-degree turn without dumping us in the bay and deftly maneuvered us under the bow of the huge forty-five-footer as it slammed ten feet in and out of the water. Big Bill stood precariously in the skiff's bow, reaching up toward the stormy skies as we rose on the apex of a wave. It took every ovary I possessed to hold the skiff steady as the monster boat came down on us. Just as the knife made contact, our skiff surged ahead and we slammed into the side of my Navy houseboat with a thud. We were now between my sixty-three-foot boat and the intruding forty-five-footer. They came perilously close to squishing us like bugs on a windshield, and then, just in the nick of time, floated apart like violent lovers transcending fatal peril.

I took a breath of air, and then another. I was still alive and well. We had played a dangerous game and won the right to go on living. In a fit of ceremonial triumph, I screamed louder than all the elements put together, *I am the Amazon Queen and I can do anything!*

kym trippsmith (mamazon@monitor.net; www.monitor.net/~ mamazon) is a writer and performance artist in Occidental, California. Her first novel, *The Plight of the Amazon Queen,* fictionalizes her real-life, wild experiences—of which you, Dear Reader, have gotten only a glimpse.

CHAPTER 5

Rebels: Individuals Taking a Stand

Having principles

UNSHAKEABLE BELIEFS

Commitment to a vision

Inevitably there will be times when we will face obstacles of the human variety: a dominant authority figure, another person's hurtful attitude, or a community's prejudicial assumption about what a girl can or can't do. Hard to ignore, these obstacles goad us. They get in the way of daily living. And their presence forces us to a crossroad: We must decide, *Will I move on—just let this one go? Or will I stand up for my beliefs?*

The women and girls in this chapter face that crossroad, and they choose to take a stand.

They believe in their ideals. They refuse to let their principles slide. They are dedicated to a vision—whether it be that the world should be rape-free or accessible to wheelchair users—and they are letting the people around them know it. By definition, rebels go against the status quo, so those in power may try to block a rebelgirl's efforts. These stories tell of females who are undeterred by the opposition they face. They challenge conditions they find oppressive and do what, to them, is the right thing—even if they meet with resistance.

If a voice goes against commonly accepted assumptions, then speaking out, in and of itself, is courageous. What is remarkable about the women and girls in this chapter is that they go beyond speaking out. They act. Most engage in risky physical activity that further commits them to their rebellion. They take a stand not just with their minds and mouths, but with their bodies.

A woman who stands up for her beliefs is often simply standing up for *herself* as an individual. If she is unaware there are others facing similar situations and, like her, taking the Action Hero route, she may feel alone. Though she may keep-on-keeping-on and use injustice as a springboard for social change (*Pow!* "Take that, supervillain!"), she may not realize until years later that her individual response was part of a greater movement of resistance and transformation.

On the other hand, rebelling can be an exhilarating awakening. An "ah-ha" moment. Maybe a woman sees for the first time how her single act fits into a larger social picture: an *ah-ha* moment of understanding the political context of her personal experience. Yup, rebelling can be a life-changing event that politicizes a girl.

Regardless of whether the women in these stories see how they fit into the bigger picture, their acts of courage have a ripple effect. When a woman wins a battle for herself, she often wins it for the girl next door, too. Though she does something on her own, her act reverberates and ultimately has wider repercussions. (That was a hint; see the chapter after this one for the ripples!)

✷ Letting Justice Flow
alison kafer

I have no legs.

One night, six years ago, I fell asleep an active, able-bodied young woman. Months later I woke up, my arms, belly, and back covered in burn scars. The legs that had carried me for years were missing, amputated above the knees as a result of my burns. The last few years have been a continual process of learning how to move and understand myself in this new, and yet old, body.

Before my disability, I saw myself as a political activist only when involved in a demonstration or protest. Now, however, I understand my very body as a site of resistance. Every single time I leave my house, people stare. Their eyes linger on my scars, my half-legs, and my wheelchair as they try to understand what happened and why I look the way I do. Their stereotypes about disability are written in their expressions of confusion and fear as they watch me pass. I am powerfully aware that merely by living life in a wheelchair, I challenge their stereotypes about what bodies look like and what bodies do. I feel like an activist just by rolling out my front door.

Sometimes, however, simply rolling outdoors isn't enough of a statement. Sometimes you have to pee outdoors, too.

Three years ago, during my first semester of graduate school, I took an exchange class at a local seminary. A month into the course, I was assigned to give a presentation on the week's readings. Halfway through class we took a break, after which I was to give my talk. I desperately had to pee, and I rolled over to the library, sure I'd find accessible toilets there. I was met only with a wall of narrow stalls—too narrow to slide my wheels into.

I dashed about campus, rolling from one building to another, hoping to find a wide stall door, muttering to myself, "There *has* to be an accessible can somewhere on this damn campus." After checking every bathroom in every building, I realized I was wrong.

What the hell was I going to do?

Going home wasn't possible because I would never make it back to school in time to give my presentation. "Holding it" also wasn't possible because . . . well, when a girl's gotta go, a girl's gotta go. I exercised my only remaining option: I went outside, searched for a dark and secluded part of campus, hiked up my skirt, leaned my body over the edge of my wheelchair, and pissed in the grass.

It just so happened that the dark, secluded place I'd found was the Bible meditation garden.

I went back to class angry. With mild embarrassment, I told the professor what had happened. I felt validated when she stopped the class to tell everyone the seminary president's name so they could write letters demanding an accessible bathroom at the school.

The next day, I, too, wrote a letter to the president informing him of both my accessibility problem and my solution. "Odds are," I wrote, "I will need a bathroom again. And I am doubtful that my 'christening' of the Bible garden is a practice you would like me to continue." In closing, I mentioned the Bible verse I'd found emblazoned on the garden wall (the one I'd practically peed on), and hoped its irony would not escape him. "Let justice roll down like waters," the words proclaimed, "and righteousness like an everlasting stream." Never before had the Bible seemed so relevant to me!

Within forty-eight hours, I had an appointment with the school president. He ushered me into his office and sat down across from me. "Before we discuss possible construction," he said, "I just want to give you a moment to share your pain."

I paused, thinking his comment a rather condescending way to begin a meeting. "I'm not in any pain," I said curtly, "I just want a place to go to the bathroom."

Our conversation could only go downhill from there.

The president informed me that although he wanted to provide me with an accessible bathroom, the school could not currently afford such construction. When I suggested that removing a forty-year-old skanky couch from one of the women's rooms would free up space for an accessible stall, he responded with a sentiment as old as the couch: "Well, I'm reluctant to remove the sofa because some of the lady students like to rest there *during their time.*"

Right. I'd forgotten how much we lady students, brains overtaxed by academia, liked to rest, bleeding, on musty couches in dank bathrooms. What a traitor to my sisters I must have been to suggest that my need to pee was more important than a couch that hadn't seen human contact since 1973.

Not surprisingly, that meeting did not result in an accessible toilet. So, as threatened, I continued to piss in the garden and complain in the halls. What had started out as a necessity became an interesting combination of necessity *and* protest—a pee protest. Word got around, and to my delight most students supported me. Petitions were signed in a number of classes. One student even proposed a documentary on *The Bathroom Debates* to her film class, showing them a short teaser clip she'd made. I became a bit of a celebrity, known in the halls as "the bathroom girl."

About a month after the first incident, I fired off another letter to the president informing him of my continued use of the Bible meditation site. This time I meant business. I told him I was ready to expose his total disregard of the needs of disabled Americans by going to the press with my story. Bingo. Construction began on the most beautiful accessible bathroom you ever did see.

Justice and righteousness were rolling down at last. They had just needed a little boost from a girl, her wheelchair, and a full bladder.

alison kafer is a graduate student in Women's Studies and Religion. In between battles with university administrators about inaccessible buildings, she kayaks, camps, and hikes. A relentless optimist, Alison insists that most people stare at her not because of her disability, but because of her southern charm and dazzling physical grace.

∞

One Moonshine Night
julia willis

My daddy had a bootlegger named Lem. His still was way up in Burke County, on the edge of the Blue Ridge Mountains, about an hour's drive on highways and backroads from where we lived. Actually, Lem was a pig farmer, but he ran a nice little moonshine business on the side. Even in the boondocks, even in the Eisenhower years, they knew it paid to diversify.

Now I was never sure whether Daddy made that trip up to Lem's every so often because he got word through the good old boys' grapevine there was a new batch of corn liquor on the cooker, or he just hightailed it back for more whenever he ran low. I knew he didn't like to be without, though I'd seen him go a month or two on the wagon after an especially grueling binge. But the particulars of Daddy's drinking was one of those things the family didn't talk about. He drank in secret, disappearing into his basement workshop several times a night to mix up and chug down his favorite combination of sweet Sundrop citrus cola and white lightning that had a kick like a mule. No one liked to mention those frequent trips downstairs or his steady evening slide into slurring, stumbling oblivion.

This was our dead elephant in the middle of the room, the one everyone tried to pretend wasn't there as they gingerly tip-toed around it. While he was in the basement, lifting another juice glass, my grandmother might make a wry comment like "What do y'all reckon Bill's working on in his shop tonight?," answering herself with "Must be mighty interesting." Everyone else would ignore her, shake their heads sadly, or paste on an ironic smile, pretending it didn't matter but praying he'd soon shuffle quietly off to bed, hoping it wouldn't be one of those nights when some little remark or gesture would set him off and turn him into a dangerous weapon. Even though he mostly took out his rage on the furniture, tossing it around the room or out the back door into the yard, there was always the stomach-churning thought that one of us might be next. And being the youngest in the family, with the least amount of practice keeping my eyes downcast and my mouth shut, I was convinced that "one" would someday be me.

Once we made it safely through those nights, with dawn came the hangovers, the regrets, and the unsolicited promises he'd "straighten up, fly right, and never do that again," without ever specifying exactly what "that" was. By the time I was old enough to know what a promise meant, I knew better than to believe in his. They only lasted as long as it took him to get thirsty again.

Sometimes Daddy took me with him to Lem's. He never told me that was where we were going. The two of us would just be up in the country paying visits to his kinfolks, and then first thing you know I'd be sitting in our old Ford in Lem's dirt driveway that overlooked the hog pen while the men took the empty jugs out of the trunk and, leaving the lid up, went off down in the woods to make the deal.

With the windows barely cracked, I sat alone, broiling in the afternoon sun. I never got out of the car because I was told not to. Besides, Lem had a couple of mangy dogs in the yard that bared their teeth to strangers. I'd know the deal was done when I heard them slam the trunk lid shut.

But finally, the summer I turned eleven, one weekend when I hadn't gone with him to Lem's, when he'd come home with a snootful which he proceeded to top off throughout the course of the afternoon and evening, leaving the furniture intact but acting awfully mean and nasty, slicing us up pretty good with cruelly barbed comments calculated to ruin everybody's Saturday night, I figured I'd had about enough.

After he'd gone to bed, leaving the rest of us breathing a collective sigh of relief, I snuck down to the workshop where he kept his gallon jugs of clear white lightning in an old wooden cabinet with sagging hinges on the doors. There were a dozen jugs in all. Two at a time, one in each hand, I carried them out the cellar door, across the yard, into the pasture, and halfway down the worn dirt path the goats made on their way to the barn. When I came to a good open spot that sloped down to the creek at the bottom of our land, I took those jugs, uncapped them, and by the light of a full moon poured that liquor on the ground. It wet down the dusty path, trickled down the slope, and gave off a powerful smell so reminiscent of Daddy's sour breath I turned around twice to see if I'd been caught. But I hadn't, so I went on hauling and pouring till I'd emptied every last jug, including the half-full one sitting on his workbench beside a carton of warm colas. I didn't leave him a single drop.

When I'd finished and put the empty jugs back where I found them, I felt righteously exhilarated, for about two minutes—until I realized I was now in serious trouble. I'd be the first one he'd suspect, and if he asked me I'd be sure, foolishly but proudly, to confess. Plainly put, I was a goner, destined to be struck down dead by my own father's hand, unless he decided to hold me over for slow torture.

Seeking absolution, before I went to bed I told my mother, who was watching Lawrence Welk and His Champagne Musicmakers, what I'd done. First stunned into silence by the magnitude of my crime, she soon recovered, secretly pleased, I imagine, that someone in the family had finally done something, and that her daughter could actually be so bold.

"Well," she said in her nonconfrontational way, "let's just wait and see what happens. Maybe he's had enough for now." Her advice was twofold: not to say anything to him about it, which was easy, and not to worry, which was hard.

I lay awake all that night, listening for him to wake up and slip down for another drink, find his jugs empty, and go berserk. I was coiled like a spring, ready to leap out my bedroom window at the first sound of slamming doors or breaking furniture. I finally dozed off at dawn, but I heard later what transpired. I was asleep, with Mother in the kitchen cooking grits and sausage, when Daddy made his first trip of the day downstairs for a "hair of the dog." In a matter of seconds he stormed upstairs again.

"Something wrong, Bill?" Mother asked him.

"You know, don't you?" he hollered. "So where the hell is it?"

"While you were sleeping," she said calmly, stirring her grits, "your daughter poured it all out in the pasture."

Daddy's mouth dropped open. "Wha—why would she do such a thing?"

Mother turned from the stove and looked him straight in the eye. "Why do you think?"

Of course, he knew the answer, so that was the end of their brief conversation about our dead elephant.

It would be nice to say that morning marked the end of his drinking, but it didn't. Daddy left the house and drove away, probably over to a drinking buddy's to get his Sunday morning miracle cure. I made sure to stay out of his way as he came and went that day, though Mother assured me he was too shocked to even discuss the matter, let alone punish me for the deed. That night we could hear him in his workshop, banging and hammering. Still waiting for the ax to fall, I imagined he was knocking together a cheap coffin to dispose of my lifeless body once he'd killed me, and after he went to bed I snuck down there again to see. He had tightened the hinges and attached Yale locks to the upper and lower doors of that cabinet where the jugs were kept. With all the doors sealed up tight, it was a pretty safe bet he'd made another trip to Lem's that afternoon with a trunkload of empty jugs, and brought them back filled. I was clearly fighting a losing battle.

Still, I reckoned we both knew where we stood on the subject of moonshine after that. I never poured his liquor out again, even when I discovered where he kept the keys to the cabinet, and he never invited me to go with him to Lem's anymore. He never did quit drinking either, till he got too old and sick, which doesn't really count. But he hasn't said a word to me about that night, not to this very day. Since we both knew where we stood, wasn't nothin' left to say.

While **julia willis,** author of the novel *Reel Time* (Alyson), comes from a long line of Southern liars and storytellers, drunks and teetotalers, she still avoids that moonshine like the plague, preferring instead a good single-malt Scotch. She now resides in Quincy, Massachusetts.

∞

Yay for Hairy Women!

mica miro

"What's taking you so long, Mica? You're not the only one who uses this bathroom!" my sister yelled, thumping on the door.

I grunted in response, too caught up in trying to twist my leg around to see the back of my calf to say more. I had shaved my legs only twice before in my whole life, and I wasn't so good at it. The first time I shaved, I got a horrible rash. One of my friends said, "Maybe you didn't use enough soap," and I thought, *Oh. Soap?* Even after I found out about the soap part, I couldn't believe girls took all that time every day just to scrap off their hair.

At my school, what no one could believe was that I *didn't* shave. In seventh grade, I was the only girl with hairy legs. I was aware of it every time I walked down the hall in shorts. My hair was (is) pretty much as dark as it gets. Most girls glanced as I walked by and, shocked, stopped talking or even whispered to their friends. They never said anything directly to me. The boys did. They flat-out asked: "What are you thinking? Why don't you just shave?" My volleyball team made fun of me, in a sweet way, I guess: "Hippie child," they'd call me, and they'd say, "You come from the woods, don't you?"

My best friends tried to convince me to shave. "You have such nice legs, you should show them off," Ashley told me as we changed for P.E.

"Yeah," Rachel chimed in, "you really should shave, Mica, it would be so much fun."

I laughed at my friends, and occasionally talked back to the boys, when I felt brave enough: "You don't shave, so why should I?"

I didn't feel as secure as I sometimes acted. In middle school it was crucial to fit in. At the same time, it was cool to be different. But you had to be different in the *right* way, a way that fit in; otherwise you were just weird. The cooler you already were, the more your being different was accepted as the *right* way. I wasn't the geekiest at my school, but neither was I cool enough to get away with being different. So my hairy legs were considered weird, even a little freakish.

In P.E. class we were required to wear shorts. I felt super self-conscious, especially since we were seated alphabetically for roll call. I was always next to this popular boy, Markos Matthews. He was flabbergasted that I didn't shave. Like all the boys, he thought it looked strange and unnatural, even gross, since every other girl he knew was waxy smooth. It was like everyone thought the other girls didn't even grow hair there. Uncomfortable in P.E., I wanted to disappear—go outside, play soccer, and forget about leg hair.

So why didn't I just shave? Well, growing up with unconventional, offbeat parents in a small, rural town, I'd gotten used to the idea of being different from other people. Besides, my mother had hairy legs, though hers were usually hidden under pants or long skirts. Also, when I was six, I had a baby-sitter who didn't shave. When I asked her why, she told me hairy legs were a wonderful thing, and that all hairy women should always be proud. With that, we took off down the street, chanting, "Yay for hairy women! Yaaay for hairy women!"

So those two times I had tried to shave, besides the awful rash, the cuts, and the way the pink Bic throwaway razor kept falling out of my hand, I also felt like something of a traitor. Yet, by the middle of seventh grade, I was also tired of feeling so uncomfortable in school. That's when I came up with my plan. I had gotten the idea from my sister's friend. He had shaved his head in stripes and everyone in their high school thought it was so cool. Of course, he was already cool to start with.

"Mica! Get out! It's my turn," my older sister banged on the door again, two hours later.

"Leave me alone. I'm almost done," I hollered back, rinsing the final suds from my legs and standing up to examine my handiwork in the mirror.

The next morning, getting ready for school, I was flooded with doubts. At the last minute I decided to wear long pants. But I still had to change into shorts for P.E. *What if I made a mistake?* I thought with dread, as I nervously walked into the gym. *What will the boys say? I have to sit next to Markos and he's going to flip out.* Then I heard someone say, "Hey Mica, what did you do? Guys, look at Mica!" Suddenly everyone crowded around to ooh and ahh.

"Is that really your hair?" one boy asked.

"Did it grow that way?" inquired another.

"Mica, that is so awesome. I would never be brave enough to do that," said Ashley.

"Hey, Mica, you are totally cool!" said Rachel, looking down.

What they were all staring at were the perfectly concentric, evenly spaced, horizontal rings of pale skin and dark hair on both of my legs, from ankle to mid-thigh. I looked like Pippi Longstocking, and it was a hit. Kids I saw every day, kids who had barely talked to me before, in part because of the dumb tension about my hairy legs, came up to tell me that what I'd done was so cool. Everyone thought it was great. I felt like the Star of the Day.

mica miro, eighteen now, attends an all women's college where there are lots of original, forward-thinkers; she is surrounded by hairy legs ("Yaaay!"). The Pippi-look, though, was a one-shot deal. "It took so long, I couldn't be bothered to do it again."

∞

Painting the Town
sasha claire mcinnes

Rewind—It's the mid-70s and I am an artist who has been invited to Ottawa to work for Status of Women Canada to provide input into a Royal Commission on Canadian Culture. I begin commuting—two weeks in my hometown in southwestern Ontario, two weeks in Ottawa.

One February night I am working late with several other women in the community. After the meeting we each go our separate ways. I walk home along the Rideau Canal to take in a bit of the Winterlude festival; the lights look lovely reflecting off the snow and ice blanketing the ground.

I am on the fringe of a group of people walking from the roadway down to the canal when I am grabbed from behind and pushed into a van. A body sits on me, and the van drives off. When it stops, there is a very deep quiet and then voices speak in a language I don't understand. I am kept in the van until the early morning of what I think is the following day, but later find out is the morning after. Finally, they push me out and into the snow, somewhere on the outskirts of Ottawa.

Fast Forward—I am back home in southwestern Ontario. It is now three months later. I have spent much of those three months in the bathtub.

One night I awake at 2:00 A.M. knowing it is time to take back my power. Time to stop blaming myself for having wanted to enjoy an Ottawa night. Time to stop believing the men who told me I was a "slut who liked to eat sh*t." Time for Sasha to really come home—to herself.

I get out of bed, shower, anoint myself with a favorite oil, tie my long hair up under a cap and go out to the garage to find what I need: a can of fluorescent pink paint, a paintbrush, and a broom handle. I tape the brush to the end of the handle and hit the streets. An enormous calm and focus envelops me as I methodically dip and brush. While I am careful to hide when a car comes along, I don't much care if I am caught. By 6:00 A.M. I have painted RAPE on five dozen stop signs all across the city.

I go home and sleep like a baby for the first time in months. I wake to an answering machine full of messages from friends ("Has our favorite uppity feminist finally resurfaced?"); to a newspaper filled with photographs of my STOP RAPE signs; and to the radio reporting traffic jams all across the city. Debates in the Letters to the Editor section of our newspaper rage for weeks.

Play—"Who did this?" *Ms. Everywoman, of course.*

"Why?" *Hmm. Let's consider all the possible reasons, shall we?*

"She ought to pay!" *News flash: She already has.*

In fact, this action was my way of saying that we all have to pay, in one way or another, for male violence against women and children.

Pause—If you are ever in a city where you see "RAPE" painted on the stop signs, remember that it was done by a woman who was taking back her power. Someone like me.

sasha claire mcinnes is an uppity tapestry weaver who grew up in Peru and now lives a bit farther north. She runs a travel company, Puchka (www.puchkaperu.com), which organizes cultural/market/textiles tours with textile artists and historians of Peru and Bolivia. Sasha believes all artists should take their craft to new heights—like eight or nine feet, the height of Canadian stop signs.

∞

Camping with a Ventilator
connie panzarino

Imagine me and three personal care assistants (PCAs) squashed into a van packed to the roof with tracheotomy supplies, extra hoses and batteries for my ventilator—upon which I am twenty-four-hour dependent—suction machines, blood pressure cuff, oxymeter to monitor oxygen and pulse, stomach care supplies for my G- and J-tubes, through which I get hydration and medications, and enough pureed food and potato buds for ten days. Plus foam mattresses, tents, sleeping bags, maps, spring- and sterile water.

I carried an "I'm gonna do this!" attitude like a banner.

For nearly twenty years I had attended the annual Michigan Women's Music Festival, where I enjoyed five days of music, hundreds of craft vendors, dozens of workshops, and the sister-hood of thousands from around the world. I even learned to camp in a tent—and I loved it.

But I was not on a ventilator then.

Because of Spinal Muscular Atrophy Type II, I am now. Basically, I can move my right thumb, and my head slightly. I have full sensation but no movement everywhere else. This year was the twenty-fifth anniversary of the festival, and the first of the new millennium. Attached to a ventilator or not, Herculean task or not, I had to go. I hadn't spent all this time trying to stay alive just to sit at home.

The music festival takes place in August, not far from Lake Michigan. Since I am able to tolerate being up and in my wheel-chair only six to eight hours at a stretch, I planned the trip from Boston carefully. On the morning of departure, I stayed on my bed and ate breakfast while PCAs and friends loaded the equip-ment into the van. I got into my chair while they packed my bed-side ventilator, then positioned myself in the van with feet elevated on pillows as they packed more equipment around me. We drove eight hours to Niagara Falls on the Canadian side. Exhausted by this leg of the journey, I planned on staying for two nights. As soon as we got to the motel, I got into the bed, spent.

The next day, the parking attendant got us a special parking spot directly across from the falls. It was crowded. But it was a clear and beautiful day, and the sun baked my skin pleasantly as the breeze and spray from the falls cooled me down. People did look at me with my big electric wheelchair, ventilator and suc-tion machine on back, but mostly they smiled and made room for me to see past them. It was a little like being an ambassador for life on a vent.

The next morning we pushed on through Canada, driving only five hours, and afterward I immediately got into bed again. Knowing I would grow more tired as the trip went on, I had planned on less and less travel each day. The last stretch was a two-hour drive to the festival itself.

When we arrived, I was given permission to drive my van into the center of the festival to unload. Usually one has to transfer to a wheelchair-accessible shuttle bus, but we just had too much stuff. I was met with hugs and kisses from old lesbian friends and exchanged greetings with new ones. "Helping Hands" from the Disabled Area Resource Tent helped us with unloading and dinner while we listened to live music playing in the background. We were tired and hot—but it was so exciting to be there. Women, some topless or comfortably nude in the heat, all bedecked in feathers, big necklaces, scarves, or other outrageously festive attire, stopped to chat as we set up our dome tents. The festival carpenters had built for me a platform bed high enough to transfer from. I put my foam mattresses on top, my plastic tubs and milk crates filled with supplies underneath. I hung bags of clothes and medications on bungee cords and set up my bedside vent.

Extra ventilator batteries were positioned by the bed, in case of a power failure. Never too careful, I had also brought a special cable that could run either vent off of any car battery. The festival provided outlets from which we ran extension cords to my tent. I plugged several power strips into them for the ventilator, battery chargers, nebulizer (for asthma), electric heater, blender, and hot pot. The hot pot was crucial; the equipment needed to be washed in hot water. I tried to keep things as sterile as possible. I had my PCAs use more gloves than usual, since it was difficult for them to wash their hands between procedures. I put my little rainbow flag in front of the path to our tents. This was our home for the next five days.

Using the vent in the tent was not much different than using it in my apartment. While traveling around enjoying crafts, concerts, parades, dances, and seven thousand women—four hundred with disabilities—I made sure I had plastic bags and ponchos to cover myself and the ventilator if it rained. I carried my ambu bag and suction machine with extra suction catheters, medications, inhalers, water, and snacks, in case I could not get back to my tent for several hours. A roll of tape and a small toolbox also lived with me.

The festival was a total success. I saw Edwina Lee Tyler, Holly Near, Rhiannon, Toshi Reagan, and others perform, bought lots of ceramics, and met with many women. I also led a workshop on Ableism, Isolation, and Networking. I ended it with a piñata party, where women had a grand old time knocking down candy with crutches and canes. I got tanned, feeling good about the fact that since we were all women, I could actually go topless. Nobody stared at the two catheters protruding from my stomach. I felt nurtured, exotic with feathers and beads in my hair, and triumphant that even though I was now trached and vent dependent, I could still be here. It was like coming home.

Life was good.

We returned to Boston with less stuff in the van, but lots of memories to carry me through the winter.

connie panzarino (www.conniepanzarino.org) is a lesbian, author, artist, disability rights activist, and psychotherapist. Her writing, including her autobiography, *The Me in the Mirror* (Seal Press), serves to educate people about ableism and homophobia. This year Connie hopes to write *the* book on ableism, buy an accessible RV, and speak her way across country. This story was adapted from an article that first appeared in *Access Expressed!*, published by VSA Arts of Massachusetts. (Rivka's note: While this book was being put to bed, Connie unexpectedly passed away. She will be sorely missed, and the difference she made with her activism will always be felt.)

∞

A Room of Our Own
kathryn roblee

In the mid-1980s, I was approaching middle age and had already put up with a lot of B.S. in my eighteen years as a tradeswoman. I was a millwright, a heavy-duty field machinist, doing ironwork for large-scale projects. To give people a better idea of my skills, I used to say, "If you want a railroad car put up on the roof, I could do that for you," including reinforcing the building structure to support the weight. At the time, I was in the construction division of a major company, and assigned to help build a new automated warehouse for them. It was to be one of the largest "under one roof" structures in the world. The company was already huge—300 buildings sprawling over eight square miles. They needed company buses to wind about this manufacturing maze: an efficient system for moving around 35,000 employees.

There were other tradeswomen in the construction division besides me. Gloria was an apprentice millwright, Deana a pipefitter, Alice an instrumentation specialist. Prudy, Susan, and Jeannie were electricians. Pat was a sheet metal apprentice. On our project, that made eight women and about four hundred men.

Portable trailers were brought in to serve the crew, including a general tool crib, offices for trade supervisors, a break room, and a restroom facility: a men's facility, that is. The fact that we women needed a restroom, too, was considered unnecessary. None of us was terribly concerned—at first. When nature called, we simply went to the back of the site, across a lot, and into a side door of an already operational wing of the warehouse. But within a few weeks, warehouse workers started complaining about our muddy-booted presence in their territory. The doors to their quadrant were soon locked.

Our recourse was to go to the corner and wait for the once-every-eleven-minute bus, which we rode for half a mile to the next completed wing. However, within two weeks we were banned from that site, too. It was getting ridiculous. Now a trip to the restroom required waiting for the once-every-fifteen-minute shuttle and a seven-mile round trip, keeping a woman off the job for up to forty minutes. We were there to work, not ride buses.

When I approached my foreman, I wasn't surprised that he

laughed at me for thinking this could possibly have enough weight to even be considered a problem. But it was, and I wouldn't leave his office.

"Kathy, I'm too busy to deal with it. Let one of the other trades' foremen."

"Nobody's dealing with it, and we still need a bathroom."

Finally he said he would bring it up at a meeting that afternoon. I was later told a solution had been found: The men and women would share the washroom facility. When a woman went in, she'd put up a sign, taking it down when she left.

The first day was tough. Men were angry about having to wait for a woman whom they felt didn't belong in their space anyway. By midafternoon, a guy came along, tore the sign off, threw it in the mud, walked in, and used the urinal while Prudy was in there. She was furious. We rinsed the sign off and tried again.

The next day, one of us, I think it was Jeannie, was in the bathroom, stopping to wash her hands, when a man came in and unzipped his pants. He pulled out his penis, jumped in front of her, and made comments that matched his actions. She ran out in shock and quickly notified the rest of us.

That was it, the last straw.

I went to my toolbox and got my safety lock. No one else except a security guard had the key, and it was considered a serious offense to ever cut a safety lock unless a department head gave his permission, so I knew this would not be treated lightly. Then I changed the sign to read WOMEN'S ROOM ON MONDAY, WEDNESDAY, & FRIDAY. MEN'S ROOM ON TUESDAY & THURSDAY. That seemed fair. I hung the sign and, it being Wednesday, snapped my lock on the door.

A fellow soon came along and demanded I let him in. I told him to wait until tomorrow. In a rage, he stormed off toward the supervisors' trailer. By the time the foremen arrived, several other men were in line. My legs trembled in front of the gathering, but I refused to remove the lock.

The other managers demanded that my foreman get me

under control. "Kathy," he fumed, "these men have to use the bathroom."

"Tell them to take the bus over to Building 165," I countered.

"You can't expect hundreds of men to go off the job like that," he snarled.

"Then tell them to wait until—" I looked over at the sign I'd written, "Thursday."

He looked at me as if I was crazy, then stormed back to his office.

But he must have done something back at that office, because the very next day a brand-new women's restroom facility was delivered. We had won.

kathryn ("Where did you say you wanted that railroad car?") **rob-lee** is retired after twenty-two years as a millwright, and feels it is important that people hear what it was like in the early days of women's doing nontraditional work. She believes that women should always stand up for themselves, even if it is on trembling legs. She resides in western New York.

∞

Davida and Goliath
jane colby

"How dare they. How *dare* they?!"

I stared in disbelief at the most recent issue of the *British Medical Journal (BMJ)*. Not one, but three articles in the prestigious periodical had publicly trashed my research. The entire medical establishment of England seemed ranged against me.

They were attempting to discredit my five-year project. The one that had studied a third of a million school pupils; a properly peer-reviewed study that had been conducted with a famous microbiologist and published in a reputable U.S. medical journal; research that when I first went public with it, took top spot on the national newspapers and TV news networks.

You don't believe it? Believe it.

Steeling myself, I sat down to flip through the pages of Britain's top medical journal. The articles on us included one by a leading pediatrician alleging research bias, and an end-piece questioning *my* personal integrity and motivation.

"Oh yeah? Right, guys. We'll see about that."

This had to be put right, and now. Sure, I thought about my reputation, but mostly I thought, *If I don't fight back, who will take the kids seriously? Who will help them if I don't?* It'd be a daunting task to take on the medical establishment. *Can I do it?* I wondered. I had to think about it—for all of one minute.

If I could survive the same horrendous illness the children had, including the years of pain and disability, and if I could survive that harrowing two-day media frenzy of last May, when I first released the research results, I sure as hell could sort this.

What was their problem? Didn't they want to know the truth?

Schools Hit by ME Plague, ran the front-page headline of Britain's leading newspaper last spring. With that, the country's top medics were caught with their pants down. That was what hurt. They should have known. They, themselves, should have done the study and fronted the cameras—not me. They didn't take it kindly, hearing it from a writer and one-time school principal. Especially when they had been denying there was any problem at all. Now, smarting, they chose to attack instead of acknowledge the truth about this disabling disease.

You're asking, What is this illness? What was all the fuss about?

I'll tell you what. We'd discovered that ME (Myalgic Encephalomyelitis), also known as Chronic Fatigue Syndrome (CFS), was much more prevalent than previously known. Our research proved that over half the country's kids on long-term sick leave had it. And yes, it is a physical illness, not an emotional one. Brain scans and other tests have proven that. Chronic Fatigue

Syndrome? It may have been given a pathetic name, and some outdated doctors may still refuse to recognize it, but ME/CFS is a devastating disease.

I know firsthand.

ME/CFS can be triggered by a number of things. I got it after contracting a viral illness related to polio. Then for twelve years I was in constant pain and bedridden, slowly moving from a wheelchair to a walking aid. I gave up my career as a school principal to concentrate on getting well. As I got stronger, I retrained myself as a journalist and, with a consultant microbiologist, spent half a decade investigating 333,000 schoolchildren. In the end, our study showed ME/CFS was the single biggest cause of long-term sick leave in British schools, bigger than cancer and leukemia combined. No other illness came close. In short, we'd found a cluster pattern, a plague, in our schools. And yes, it exists in the United States, and in South Africa, Europe, Australia, Japan, wherever. Thousands upon thousands of kids have it. Most of them aren't listened to or believed when they say they are too exhausted to move, too brain fogged to think clearly, or in too much body pain to go to school.

But we listened. That was why we did the study. That was why I now couldn't ignore the attacks. No one would take our work seriously if the *BMJ* said it was flawed. So I set out to make them admit it wasn't. I began a campaign to get Goliath, Britain's medical establishment, to acknowledge the health crisis at hand.

First we sent a strongly worded complaint stating they had published incorrect information. We backed up our claim with data proving the accuracy of our research. Then we threatened "further action" if a published correction and apology were not given. I followed up with resolute and persistent phone calls.

It took six months, but finally, once again, I was staring in disbelief at the prestigious *BMJ*. This time it was what I *wanted* to see. My tenacity had paid off: *Journal Was Wrong to Criticize Study in Schoolchildren,* ran their headline.

With that apology, our research was affirmed, thereby helping the country realize the critical role ME/CFS played in our children's health. In addition, I, as co-researcher, was recognized; I was made a member of the UK Chief Medical Officer's Working Group, as well as Children's Officer for a noted national charity. But the icing on the cake came the day the esteemed pediatrician who had originally attacked me in the *BMJ* now publicly introduced me.

"We know," he said, "that ME/CFS is responsible for more long-term sickness absence in schoolchildren than any other disease. One of the authors of the paper is sitting here beside me."

I smiled and got ready to speak.

jane colby (jane@youngactiononline.com) is author of *ME–The New Plague* and *Zoe's Win*, a family book on ME/CFS (both with Dome Vision). She supports sick children through her work with Tymes Trust in Essex, England. This international organization works in partnership with www.youngactiononline.com, Jane's website, which has free info on ME/CFS. Together they send a free quarterly e-zine (e-Tymes) to their overseas members. Jane no longer uses a walking aid; she now simply floats along on her solid reputation.

For additional information on Chronic Fatigue Syndrome, contact:
The CFIDS Association of America
P.O. Box 220398
Charlotte, NC 28222-0398
Toll-free Info Line: (800) 442-3437
Resource Line: (704) 365-2343
Fax: (704) 365-9755
E-mail: info@cfids.org.
Website: www.cfids.org

∞

Taking Up Tools
elizabeth young

When I was growing up, no one could get away with telling me I couldn't do something "because you're a *girl*." In fact, if someone wanted me *not* to do something, that was the worst thing they could say: It practically guaranteed I'd run out and try to do it.

One summer day shortly after high-school graduation, my father asked me if I had any male friends who wanted to make a bit of money. Doing what, I inquired. Helping him shingle the roof, he replied. Immediately I bristled. "Why does it have to be a male friend? Why not *any* friend, even a female one?"

My father looked surprised. "Because it's carpentry," he defended himself. "I need a helper who can do hard work and isn't afraid to get dirty."

"What! A girl could do that, too, you know. It's not a male prerogative." My own father. I was incensed.

"Fine," my father challenged. "You help me then."

Whoops. Walked right into that one, didn't I?

Now I was stuck. I did think girls could help shingle roofs, but I hadn't meant myself specifically. I was a skinny, fragile-looking girl who generally lacked athletic skills. And at that time I was even weaker than normal. The whole reason I was around the house that summer was because I was recovering from a bout of mononucleosis. Mono had sapped so much of my energy that a recent attempt at nature-walking with some friends resulted in their having to carry me back.

But even at the best of (healthy) times, there was something more—I was afraid of heights. Anytime I got too far off the ground, my knees wobbled, my mind spun, beads of sweat sprung up all over my sticky back. My phobia was so bad I couldn't go over a bridge or climb a ladder without visualizing in disturbing detail my flailing body plummeting to an ugly death. And my fear made me shake, making it even more likely that I would fall.

Exhaustion and vertigo—not a great combo for roofing.

I knew my father would let me back down, but then I'd look as if I was just shooting my mouth off. Pride? Ego? Pigheaded-ness? "When can we start?" I asked.

In the beginning, it was plain that my dad did not expect me to last long. He wanted a helper to carry shingles up onto the roof, while he stayed on top and nailed them in. For anyone who hasn't lifted roofing shingles before, I can tell you that they are extremely heavy and awkward to carry—unless you have bulging arm muscles and a strong back. Then you could simply throw a whole package of them over your shoulder and haul it all up the ladder at once. Not me. I could only carry a few individual shingles at a time and still manage a free arm to hold on to the ladder. But my dad was stubborn enough to let me keep going until I gave up, and I was stubborn enough to refuse to stop the job I started.

Of course the first time I got high up, my whole body shook, dangerously rocking the aluminum ladder I was standing on. My dad helped me wedge the ladder extra-tightly, and then with trepidation I tried again. *Hey, I can make it up,* I discovered, *as long as I don't look down.*

In the end, we were both impressed. I was sore and tired, but kept up enough of a pace that eventually I loaded so many shingles on the roof I could even join my dad in nailing them in. (To ease my mind, we tied a rope around my leg and anchored it to the roof.) To my surprise, the work was satisfying and my fear of heights began to recede. To my father's surprise, not only did I get all the shingles onto the roof, but I was also quite good at installing them.

What began as a simple challenge bore fruit for many years. My dad retired when I was in university, and together we started a home carpentry and renovation summer business. It lasted three years. We received so many jobs through referrals from happy customers that we didn't even need to advertise.

During those years, I was continually amazed at how many old stereotypes people still applied to the carpentry field. On jobs and in supply stores my very presence brought everything from raised eyebrows to outright stares. I got the impression that many men thought the ability to use power tools was linked somehow to the Y chromosome. Several dismissed me as a "Tool Time Girl" (thanks sooo much, Tim Allen, for having scantily clad women hand you tools on your TV show). "You don't look like a carpenter," is something I heard a lot (in other words, you are too pretty, too femme).

When men told me that I don't look strong enough to do the "masculine," physical side of the work, I smiled sweetly and said, "Like any highly skilled carpenter, I sometimes hire unskilled help to assist with heavy manual labor. Are you looking for a job?"

Unfortunately, many women I've worked for are just as guilty of gender-typing the work. They exclaim, "It's just great you won't have to rely on a man to do stuff around the house." But they make no effort to learn how to do it themselves.

Women, put your hammer where your mouth is! Take up your tools! Believe me, if I can do it, you can, too.

elizabeth young (lava__beth@hotmail.com), no longer a carpenter by profession, is still a proud handywoman who digs power tools ("Pass the saber saw, please"). As for her phobia of heights, rock climbing is now her favorite hobby—from inside the gym to outdoors in New Zealand and Thailand. Her home base is Toronto, Canada.

∞

Just Don't Do It
adrienne

Last year I was in kindergarten. After reading time, the gym teacher, Scott, would take us outside to play. He had us play dodgeball in two courts, the girls' court and the boys' court. He said it wouldn't be fair if we all played together since boys were stronger than girls. That made me mad. I'm very strong, stronger than a lot of boys, but Scott made me play with the girls anyway.

One day when Scott told the girls to go to the other court, I said *no*.

I said I was going to play dodgeball with the boys. Scott got angry and said if I didn't go to the girls' court, he'd send me to the principal's office.

I still said no.

It was scary because I had never been in trouble before, and I felt bad, but I still wanted to play dodgeball with the boys.

Sitting in a corner in the principal's office, I started to cry. Principal K asked what was wrong. I told her Scott wasn't letting me play dodgeball with the boys because I was only a girl. I told her how much I wanted to play with the boys, but that Scott got mad when I asked, and then got me in trouble. Principal K said Scott wasn't being fair. She took me back outside to my class and told Scott he had to let us play in whatever game we wanted.

After that I got to play dodgeball with the boys every day, and Scott couldn't stop me just because I was a girl. I know that girls are as good as boys. If anybody tells me they aren't, I won't believe them, because they are liars. None of them can stop me from doing what I want to do.

adrienne, a five-year-old athlete, thanks her cousin, Erika, for helping her write this story.

∞

Transforming Hate
krissy

I drive on I-90 almost every day on my way to work. There has always been a lot of graffiti at one particular spot where a suburban road crosses over the interstate highway. Last summer someone spray-painted some anti-Jewish B.S. on the cement embankment, including some Nazi swastika-shaped designs.

The first time I saw it, I almost drove off the road, I was so stunned. *Surely,* I thought, *the state police or someone will sandblast it off.* But more than a month went by and it was still there.

I was raised Irish-Catholic, taught to do what needs to be done. It was Mom: She drummed into us kids that "we cannot allow ourselves to forget that we had to come to this country because we were oppressed and starving. And don't," she'd always say, "forget your neighbor who might need a hand, too." I don't know, I just never saw my mom too tired, or too timid, to do the right thing. So when no one seemed to be getting rid of that crap, I decided to do it myself.

I got some paint and rollers together, grabbed a friend, parked on the side of the highway next to the graffiti, and painted over it. Cars slowed down as they drove by, but no cops or troopers showed up. Just in case, my friend had worked out a plan for media and bail. But I didn't care; I was only interested in getting that hateful message gone.

A couple of weeks went by before another anti-Semitic message with even more obvious swastika shapes appeared. This time I didn't wait a month. We decided it was dangerous to park on the busy highway (like we had last time), so for this second round, we drove on the street that crossed the highway and parked near the bridge. We walked along the road, climbed a high fence, and hiked down a steep hill to where the graffiti was. We painted over the hate-speech and transformed the scary designs into flower shapes. While my friend returned to the car, I walked to the highway overpass. I fished my arm through the guardrail and fence and wrote SHALOM in big letters on the overpass. Now all the cars drive under a big greeting of peace.

krissy says she was raised by a wonderful, working-poor, Irish-Catholic woman who taught her to care deeply about this world, not just in thought but in action.

∞

Digging for Dough

amy richards

Gloria Steinem refers to fund-raising as the second-oldest profession—that is, second to the other great female industry, prostitution. Interestingly enough, both sex and money have historically been considered "unfeminine" and not good for "good girls." Besides the fact that sex and money were to be restricted to men, most of us were taught they were simply private matters. Weren't we all told that it's rude to ask someone how much money they make?

Well, I guess I'm rude, since I spend a good deal of my time and energy asking for, raising, and learning the real power of money. But then again, I understand these things as necessities in making social justice a reality.

I came to the task of asking people for money (because, really, that's what fund-raising is) entirely by accident. I was cofounding the Third Wave Foundation, a national organization for young feminist activists, and working on our inaugural project: fanning 120 organizers across the country to register voters in underserved communities. Mid-organizing, it became apparent we needed about $100,000 to execute the project.

$100,000.

Still stuck with the false image of what good girls were *not* supposed to talk about, I began timidly. I naïvely called businesses rumored to support good causes (like Ben and Jerry's) and wrote letters to friends, friends' parents, and former employers, asking for small sums. Once I saw the results, however, I quickly changed my tune. When I realized how much money was out there to give, and that if someone wasn't giving it to something *I* believed in, it would be money "wasted," I unabashedly started asking for more.

I called Susan, a friend and mentor, and asked her to lunch. Yes, I hesitated to cross this money boundary with her. I'd witnessed how money could split friendships. But with salad greens likely stuck between my teeth, I screwed up my nerve and said, "I know you know about our work at the Third Wave, and that you've given your commitment to similar causes in the past. I was hoping you would now support *us* as well."

"In what way?" she asked.

Ugh. Why wasn't she making this easy on me?

Just as I was about to lose my gumption and minimize the support I was requesting to a simple verbal acknowledgment, I blurted out, "How about $10,000?"

"Why didn't you ask sooner?" was her response.

After that, I got greedy. When I noticed how much people were giving to other institutions—the opera, their alma maters, and so forth—I blatantly challenged them to put their money where their politics and conscience were. And not only did I ask rich strangers, I also challenged my working- and middle-class friends.

"It's not that you don't have the money, it's that you are choosing to spend it differently. For instance, I know that your dinner out with friends cost $30, and your Kate Spade bag, about $300."

Yes, I actually said that. I figured the people who spend $10,000 a year on their country-club memberships could afford to give more than that, and, similarly, the people who spend $20 on a Gap tee shirt could commit at least that much to a good cause. In fact, the majority of contributions I've received come from people earning less than $25,000 a year.

Whereas I used to think that money wasn't something "good girls" talked about, let alone asked for, I now know that good girls don't accomplish much in life. Better yet, let me redefine the term: Good girls are those who make good things happen. So, if I haven't convinced you to drop the belief that women shouldn't talk cash, and to become a fund-raiser yourself, then at least I hope I've convinced you to give to whatever cause is dear to your heart. Or perhaps, what's dear to mine: The Third Wave Foundation, a National Organization for Young Feminists, 116

East 16th Street, 7th Floor, New York, N.Y. 10003 (www.
thirdwavefoundation.org). The power you'll gain is not a result
of the amount you give, but rather from the simple act of giving.

amy richards (amy@manifesta.net), contributing editor to *Ms.*
magazine and cofounder of the Third Wave Foundation, wants you to
be bad in the name of being good. Her latest book is *Manifesta:
Young Women, Feminism, and the Future* (Farrar, Straus & Giroux).
Find out more at www.manifesta.net.

∞

Stage Presence
phoebe eng

Growing up in the '70s in a suburb of Long Island, all I wanted
to do was fit in. For most teenagers, that was hard enough. But
for the Engs, the only Asian-American family in our little all-
American town, fitting in was a full-time vocation. It meant
learning how to act "truly American"—something that was very
important to us, and something I thought I had achieved. That's
why I tried out for my high-school play.

It was 1976, the bicentennial year, and my school decided
Oklahoma! was the perfect musical to celebrate it. After all,
Oklahoma! was all about manifest destiny, the American farmer
and the cowboy, and all that was good and pure in this great
land of ours. These sentiments were especially embodied in
Laurie and Curly, the romantic leads.

The play's patriotism was lost on me, as it was on every girl
my age. All I knew was that the annual musical was the biggest
event my high school had to offer, and if I could get the girl's
lead role, I would be set for the rest of high school. Leads were
instantly popular. For one year, I wouldn't just "fit in," I would
be the equivalent of a homecoming queen.

Five rounds into the tryouts, I found myself onstage, one of the last three girls up for the lead of Laurie, the ingénue. After the tough competition between Jean O'Callaghan, Stephanie Finkel, and me, I got it.

But I guess not everybody was quite ready for me to play the lead. There were rumblings. At a PTA meeting some very vocal parents questioned the choice.

"Can a little Asian girl really play the part that Shirley Jones played in the movie?"

"So many other girls, with nice voices and pretty blond hair, can play the role, too, can't they? Won't it be a little unconvincing if the lead is . . . Chinese?"

"It's a bicentennial year, and this, well, this is un-American!"

Up to that point, I thought I had succeeded in being all-American. I thought I was hot dogs, apple pie, and Chevrolets. I mean, I had been trying for so long. It never occurred to me that I shouldn't be entitled to what every girl in my high school wanted. Now I suddenly saw that no matter how hard I tried to fit in, no matter how much I deserved the part, some people would continue to see me as different, as "foreign."

It was hard to hear those comments. I made believe they didn't hurt, swallowed hard, and tried not to embarrass myself by crying. I felt I couldn't share these feelings with anyone—not my best friend, not even my family. *They'd never understand,* I thought. Mom and Dad had worked hard and sacrificed so much, just so this kind of thing wouldn't happen. Telling them would break their hearts.

At fourteen years old, I wasn't equipped to deal with this. I had no sudden revelations, like, for example, that the parents who voiced those concerns were narrow-minded and silly. I didn't have the chutzpah to defend myself against the PTA parents. (Not until I went to college at Berkeley did I learn the skills of protest and defiance.)

What I *did* do was go on with the show. I didn't let anyone stop me from getting up on that stage and showing everyone that, Chinese or not, I could play a magnificent Laurie. After all,

I knew I could sing. I knew I was being given a chance to shine. By showing up to rehearsal every day, in the midst of some parents' misgivings, I would defeat those comments that had tried to defeat me. In doing so, I learned a valuable lesson. Not every act of defiance is an "in-your-face" act of a fierce girl. Sometimes just sticking to your guns and not buckling under pressure can be the most radical and transforming thing one can do.

So I played that lead; I sang it loud. I made sure my entire Eng family—including aunts, uncles, and cousins—sat right in the middle of the auditorium for the rest of the community to see. On those three glorious nights, my little Long Island town got a glimpse not only of what America was, but, more important, what it could be.

phoebe eng (www.phoebeeng.com), a best-selling author (*Warrior Lessons: An Asian American Woman's Journey Into Power*, Pocket Books), has since learned a lot about speaking up. She is an award-winning community and business leader whose work focuses on leadership, corporate social responsibility, identity issues, and Asian-American women. Phoebe resides in Manhattan and now makes a living by getting up in front of packed international audiences and telling it like it is.

∞

Remaining Whole Behind Bars
fauziya kassindja

If you come to the United States seeking political asylum, you might be surprised—I was. Upon arrival you may be placed in prison-like detention. In fact, the U.S. Immigration and Naturalization Service (INS) sometimes uses American prisons to hold its detainees, including people who are escaping persecution, fleeing for their physical safety, or even their lives. People like me.

I was seventeen and living in Togo, my homeland in West Africa, when my aunt told me one morning, "You're getting married today." She pointed to the beautiful gown and jewelry she had laid out on the bed.

"What?" I shouted. Apparently it had all been arranged behind my back.

"And your husband wants you circumcised, after the wedding."

"No, please," I pleaded. "You can't do this to me!"

But she could. My aunt and uncle had legal guardianship over me now that my father had passed away and they had banished my mother from our home. I was terrified. Not only was I to marry a man I barely knew, a man twice my age with three wives, but also I was slated to have my genitals cut.

A harmful traditional practice among some African, Asian, and Middle Eastern cultures, female genital mutilation (FGM) is performed on about 2 million infants, girls, and women each year. That's more than five thousand a day. Depending on the local custom, you will either "only" have your clitoris cut off, or you will lose the whole thing, including labia minora and majora. If it is the latter, you are sewn up, leaving a small hole, hardly big enough to allow pee and menstrual blood to squeeze out. Then, with each baby you birth, you are recut and resewn anew. The rationale behind FGM is complex: It is tradition; it is thought to protect virginity and prevent promiscuity; uncircumcised females are considered dirty; girls must be cut as a requirement for marriage; and circumcised girls and woman are deemed more sexually desirable.

The practice of FGM subjects women to a number of long-term physical and psychological problems. Often carried out without anesthesia and with unsterilized razors or knives, it is a sometimes deadly practice. My other aunt died from it, as do many girls every year, either from hemorrhaging or infection.

I wanted nothing to do with either the marriage or the so-called circumcision, so with the help of my sister, and my mother from afar, I fled that very day.

But all that is just background. My story here is about something else entirely. It isn't about how I thought America would be my refuge, or how I arrived at the Newark airport and asked for political asylum, or how I was sent to prison instead, to wait (wait and wait and wait, like other refugees) until a judge could hear my case. No, my story is about resistance and holding on to one's Self in the face of cruelty, and it goes like this. . . .

Kim was evil. She was the corrections officer on duty the night I was brought, shackled, straight from the New Jersey airport to prison. She was the one who conducted my strip search, the first of many. I had my period at the time, and now, naked and humiliated, I meekly asked, "What should I do with my [soiled] pad?" She ignored me, until I asked again. Then she barked, "Why don't you *eat it.*"

That was Kim.

Kim worked the night shift. When she did her midnight count she didn't just come into our dorm cell and count bodies; she pinched, slapped, and startled each sleeping woman, one at a time. Kim.

I had been in prison a few weeks already and had come to know the million rules, including "No showering before 6:00 A.M. wake up." So, like the others, I didn't. But I did get up at 5:00 to recite Muslim words and wash parts of my body in preparation for first prayer. It was an important ritual in my religion, and something I had done every day since I was a child. Kim was still on night duty at 5:00 A.M., and one morning she rushed into our cell screaming, not caring that women around her were sleeping.

"Turn that water off! No showering until six."

Surprised, I looked up at her, "I'm not showering, I'm preparing for prayer."

I was nowhere near the shower; she could see that. I was standing in a totally separate location, at the sink, with all my clothes on, washing and silently reciting holy words.

Kim, ugly with anger, stormed toward me, turned off the water faucet, and left. I was almost finished, so I turned the water back on.

"Turn it off, I said," she yelled.

I was done by then, so I did.

The next morning, when I began my washing prayer, she rushed into the room, "Off!"

Again, I was obviously fully dressed. "But it's for my prayers." *She has to understand there is someone called God, and she must have heard about prayer,* I thought.

"No showering until six."

I stayed cool, unruffled: "I'm washing for prayer. I'm not *showering.*"

"No *washing* until six."

She was changing the rule. There may have been a million rules, all meant to control prisoners' every move, but this one was about showering, not washing. I stood my ground. God was too important to me to stop my prayers for a whimsical change of the rules. *I'll ignore her,* I thought. *She's just being mean, as usual.*

"I'm sorry. To pray, this is what I have to do."

Kim thought differently. She grabbed me, handcuffed me, and snarled, "I'm taking you to seg."

Segregation. My prison friends, loving and generous women who were more seasoned than I, had warned me about it, told me I never wanted to experience it.

She brought me through a dizzying number of hallways, opened one of the many metal doors, pushed me into a tiny cell, and locked me up, alone, in a concrete box. A metal bed, sink, and toilet, no more. No phone calls, no TV, no contact with humanity. The miniscule window on the door was too small to see anything. *Where am I? Is this the America I'd heard so much about?*

I was stunned, horribly scared, and cold. The cell was freezing, the lighting harsh. I couldn't stop thinking, *This can't be. How long will it last; how long will they keep me here? A few hours maybe; then they'll let me out. Right?* With nothing to do, my mind whirled round and round, *Why? Why? What did I do?*

I was being punished, but I had no idea for how long. *Hours, days, two weeks, a month?* I was served three meals a day, but besides that had no way of telling the passage of time. Lights off, day one ended. Lights on, day two began. I tried to convince myself that I didn't exist. It was too painful to fathom what was going on. *Okay, I'm not here.* I cried so much there was nothing left inside. I was hollow. Day three, four, then five, and they came to get me. Five days, long enough to bring me close to madness.

I later found out I was lucky. Isolation can last months, even years, in American prisons, sometimes as a form of punishment, often for seemingly arbitrary things. Like being forgotten. I don't know for sure if I *was* forgotten, but it certainly seemed that way. It happened when I was eighteen; after an inconclusive TB test, the prison quarantined me. They locked me in a tiny room and seemed to forget I existed. I was scared for my life.

Am I sick? Shouldn't they be giving me medicine? They passed meal trays through a slot in the door, but nobody would talk to me. No one explained what was going on. Days and days of being alone passed. *What kind of bad dream is this? Am I going to wake up?* Weeks went by, and my time in that cell turned into a complete blank. I remember only bits and pieces, like when I stood in front of the metal sheet that passed as a prison mirror and watched myself say, "Oh, Fauziya, you're not going crazy. Everything will be okay," only to hear myself demand a minute later for God to take me, *take me now!* I flipped back and forth between elation and despair, out-of-control laughter and sobs. *I'm definitely going out of my mind.* Finally, after I lost it and screamed my head off, they let me out. It'd been twenty days of crazed, mind-numbing isolation—something no one should have to go through.

Earlier, when I was released from my *first* experience in isolation (the five-day stint for washing), my heart was filled with hatred. I was brought before a prison official.

"Number Seven Six One?"

"Yes." I was so nervous.

"You broke the rules and fought with an officer," he said.

What? Not true, but the truth—justice—didn't count in prison.

"Your sentence is five days in segregation. You have already served your sentence. Return to your dorm."

The prison official didn't let me say anything. But I was free to go back to my dorm, back to my cellmates.

The very next morning I was up at 5:00 A.M. *The fact that I am in prison doesn't mean you can stop me from praying.* I turned the water on just a trickle and washed as quietly as I could. Maybe Kim heard, maybe not. From then on that was how I washed for prayers every morning. I was scared of being caught and taken to isolation again, yet at the same time I didn't want them to win. I was willing to take the risk; my religion was a big part of who I was, part of my Self and not something I would easily give up. I now knew if they sent me back, I might go crazy but I wouldn't die—and I could still continue to pray in there.

It took sixteen months before I won political asylum. In a landmark, precedent-setting decision, I was the first woman to be granted asylum by the INS's Board of Immigration Appeals for fleeing a forced genital mutilation. Now, when I look back, I think something must have gotten into me in prison. All the things I did, I don't know how I did them. I often think, "Gosh, I really did that?" The answer is always the same: *Yes, that strong woman is me!*

fauziya kassindja now attends college and lectures around the globe. This story was written with Rivka after an interview, and contains adapted excerpts from *Do They Hear You When You Cry* by Fauziya Kassindja and Layli Miller Bashir. Copyright © 1998 by Fauziya Kassindja. Used by permission of Dell Publishing, a division of Random House Inc. Fauziya can be contacted through Equality Now (see below).

To learn about the movement to end the human rights abuse known as female genital mutilation, contact:

Equality Now
P.O. Box 20646
Columbus Circle Station
New York, NY 10023
Phone: (212) 586-0906
Fax: (212) 586-1611
E-mail: info@equalitynow.org.
Website: www.equalitynow.org

and

The World Health Organization
Department of Women's Health
Avenue Appia 20, 1211 Geneva 27
Switzerland
Phone: (41 22) 791 21 11
Fax: (41 22) 791 3111
E-mail: info@who.int
Website: www.who.int

To get info on prison reform, contact:

Prison Activist Resource Center
P.O. Box 339
Berkeley, CA 94701
Phone: (510) 893-4648
Fax: (510) 893-4607
E-mail: parc@prisonactivist.org
Website: www.prisonactivist.org

CHAPTER 6

Doing It Together: Collective Activism

AGITATORS UNITING

Rising up, resisting, revolting

Making a ruckus

Personal commitment to a cause can take you far . . . but the fun really starts when you have a whole Babe Brigade at your side. Besides that, you accomplish more with a posse.

When a woman pools her talents with the energy of others, her ability to effect change increases exponentially. Most important, she is taken more seriously. One woman hangs out her window banging on a pot, everyone thinks she's a wacko. Twenty do it, and people know something's afoot.

These stories are about women and girls taking direct action with the support of a group. Estrogen-powered activism. When a legion of girls believes in a cause, an individual's personal beliefs and sense of power are affirmed; her conviction that *Of course I will have an impact* grows. Optimism and hope can make—or lack of it can break—a movement. Working with others can also heighten understanding of the situation, offering both a reality check (sometimes difficult to obtain working alone) and an awareness of how the act fits into the larger scheme of things.

As these stories illustrate, collective activism can be born out of the incredible bravery of a single female. Her independent rebellion gives rise to a larger one. So, in a sense, the division between the preceding chapter and this one is porous. They both show that when it comes to the end result—social change—the line between individual and collective activism blurs. Individual protests will have an impact on the larger society. And the general zeitgeist will influence individuals who are unaware a movement is stirring, yet who independently decide to take a stand regarding some personal belief.

In these stories we see the varied roles a girl agitator can play within a group. The ringleaders relay how their one match starts a bigger fire. Others are early participants, adding dry twigs to make the flame grow. Some sign on later, blowing oxygen and bringing the fire to a roaring blaze.

Whatever role a woman plays in an effort to provoke change, it is important. Whether she immediately succeeds is less so—because she can always try again! And with so many other riot-girls involved, who'd want to miss the party?

Love Thy Neighbor with Avengeance
jessica brown

I am a member of the Washington, D.C., Lesbian Avengers, a nonviolent, direct-action group of lesbian, bisexual, and trans-gender women organizing for dyke survival and visibility. For anyone not familiar with the Lesbian Avengers, we were founded in 1992 in New York City as a space for queer women to be active outside traditional male-dominated (and by extension, often sexist) political groups. By *direct action* we mean the mobilization of bodies in the streets: marching and picketing versus letter writing or lobbying. Our actions usually combine civil disobedience with equal parts street theater. We don't apply for permits because we don't ask permission. We take our shirts off at demonstrations because our bodies are not obscene.

We offer women a much-needed opportunity to kick that "nice girls don't" socialization in the ass.

Still, we aren't without our soft, romantic side either. To illustrate this, let me tell you about an action we did one Valentine's Day at the Family Research Council (FRC). The FRC is a conservative Christian organization based in D.C. They lobby the federal government for a return to legally imposed "family values." In other words, a rollback of most of the legislative and social gains made by gays, lesbians, and straight women in the last thirty years. Just before our action, FRC had also announced that it would raise money to put a series of advertisements on television claiming that homosexuality is a dangerous disease, and that gays and lesbians can be "healed" by becoming born-again Christians.

Is it any wonder that we wanted to send them a little love?

On Friday, February 12, a small group of Avengers walked into the FRC building's main lobby. About half of us were dressed like cupids. We were wearing pink gauze wings, little white tutus, and combat boots. We were, for the most part, bare breasted. Considering it was February, this was something of a chore, but we had never seen a fully clothed cupid, and we are nothing if not sticklers for authenticity. Besides, the FRC believes that modesty, chastity, and a graceful submission to her lawfully wedded husband are the chief virtues of a woman, and, well, we don't. We also brought with us a bouquet of flowers and a large red valentine heart that read:

DEAR FRC,
LOVE IS A HUMAN RIGHT.
XXOO,
THE LESBIAN AVENGERS

For a second after we burst through the double doors, the crowd in the lobby stood frozen, blinking in shock. Then the women, Republican ladies in pumps and large bulletproof hairdos, scattered, most of them making a break for the exits. Suddenly, the men were all rushing forward, demanding in loud voices that we leave immediately.

I addressed one: "Hello," I said pleasantly. "We're from the Washington, D.C., Lesbian Avengers."

"You have to leave," he informed me.

"Okay," I said. "But see, we have this Valentine for Mr. Donovan." At the time, Donovan was FRC's executive vice president; their previous director, Gary Bauer, had recently left FRC because he decided to run for U.S. president in 2000. "Is Mr. Donovan here?" I asked.

"If you don't leave right now I'm calling the police," he screamed.

"Right," I said. "But see, I made this Valentine . . ."

While I was chatting with the man, some of the Avengers attempted to make friends with the other people in the lobby. Kim, a member of our group, walked up to one of the remaining women and tried to hand her some flowers. The woman refused with a nervous smile and a shake of her head. Kim persisted. "Look," she said, "they're just flowers. For you. Take them."

The woman may have thought this was a trick. Perhaps she believed we had found a way to infect tulips with some insidious virus liable to leave her with bizarre urges to let her leg hair grow or vote Democrat. Maybe she just thought she was being asked out on a date, but for whatever reason she staunchly refused her present.

"Here. I'll just put them here." Kim bent down to leave the flowers on the floor, a foot in front of the frozen woman, then backed away very slowly.

The FRC menfolk, security and staff members, were not willing to call the police and wait the extra ten minutes for the authorities to remove us. We were a cancer that had to be excised immediately. The men grabbed us and started pushing us toward the front doors. We took that as our cue to leave. We turned to one another and had a quick kiss-in in the lobby before being shoved out onto the sidewalk. One of the staff members followed us outside to engage in dialogue: He pronounced us "sick," took our big red valentine heart and broke it over his knee, three or four times. When the pieces became too small to crack apart with his hands, he threw them down on the ground and started stomping on them, grinding the foamboard pieces into the concrete with his shoes.

Some people you just can't reach, I guess. Still, we felt better having made the effort. We continued our kiss-in on the sidewalk for a while, and then went home.

jessica brown, lesbo extraordinaire from Madison, Wisconsin, usually doesn't require a costume to fight homophobia, but on special occasions it's fun to dress up (or down, as the case may be).

∞

High-School Gauntlet
rachel

In my high school there is a patio area where everyone hangs out in between classes and during lunch. The school is small, so you can see everyone from the benches at the end of the patio. That is where the most popular boys in the school used to sit. Every day, as each girl passed, these boys stared at her and rated her different body parts from one to ten. The girls dreaded walking out of the lunchroom. This practice had been going on for years and I'm pretty sure that's why our school had one of the highest eating-disorder rates in the state.

I was friendly with these boys. I knew them all, and actually I was always glad about that because even though they still rated me, at least they never publicly humiliated me by yelling out the numbers. Until one day.

"Six."

"What? No way. That's Rachel. Eight."

"Ha! Seven for the bottom, five and a half for the top."

I felt so degraded and worthless I spent the rest of the lunch period hiding in the bathroom.

But something else happened that day, too. The girls at my school, girls who were usually so competitive with and cruel to one another, started talking. It began in the bathroom, when I rallied us together by suggesting we take action against these boys.

The next day at lunch a bunch of us girls got to the "boys' bench" before they did. We sat and waited until they approached, and when they did we called out *their* ratings as they walked by. We had it all planned out: When they came up to us to talk, we lifted their shirts and grabbed at them just the way they did to us every day. Then we handed each a letter I'd written and gotten 158 girls to sign. It said they needed to stop their behavior right away and that we were not going to stand for it any more.

It sounds amazing, but from then on it all stopped. Instead of taking their intimidating places on the bench, the boys mingled in the lunchroom. If any of the guys made any angry or sexual comments toward us about what we had done, they were immediately silenced by their friends.

It feels great knowing I did something good for girls, especially something that will help those who have yet to enter the frightening halls of high school.

rachel is a high-school junior who loves the idea of a book that celebrates women.

∞

Synagogue Revolt
loolwa khazzoom

Loolwa's note: When most of us think of "Jews," we think of Ashkenazim—*Jews from northern Europe. Jews, in fact, are an international people, with numerous ethnic groups. One such group is*

Mizrahim—Jews indigenous to the Middle East and North Africa. As a result of European racism and its internalization, Mizrahim have lost much of their heritage over the past fifty years. Even in Israel, a Middle Eastern country that until recently had a majority population of Mizrahim, Ashkenazi racism has nearly destroyed Mizrahi identity.

I was fourteen when I led the revolt. For each of the previous nine years, my family had made pilgrimage from San Francisco to Los Angeles for the Jewish High Holy Days to attend the only Iraqi synagogue this side of New York. This was the third year the new, young, Moroccan rabbi was there, leading services alongside our beloved Iraqi cantor and scholar. I walked into the synagogue with apprehension.

Everyone in my family hated the new rabbi. He may have been Mizrahi, but like many who have internalized the dominant culture, he acted Ashkenazi. "What is he doing in an Iraqi synagogue anyhow?" my parents would mutter. "He's no Iraqi."

For the past two years, the young rabbi and two Israeli congregants—all with booming voices—had taken over the singing, drowning out classic Mizrahi songs and replacing them with Ashkenazi-Israeli songs. Both years, everyone had submitted to the takeover, in typical fashion of the passive Iraqi Jew, by either joining in with these traitors to our culture or simply not resisting. I ached inside, watching the sad faces on old Iraqi men as they quietly gave up singing, removed their prayer shawls, and headed home.

Both years, I felt helpless. Trapped in the back of the synagogue, I hung over the top of the four-foot wall separating the women from the men, and sang Mizrahi songs at the top of my lungs. But my young voice alone was no match for the traitors' powerful pipes. I felt desperate and powerless.

My eyes always faced forward into the men's section, where the action happened and the power lay. *I belong up there,* I thought to myself every time I attended synagogue. *They should have me up there leading.* I knew all the prayers, largely by heart. I sang in the traditional Iraqi way, with the distinct Iraqi pronunciation of each word. In the United States, where I was raised, it was unusual for adults to preserve the Mizrahi traditions, and unheard of for youth to know them. But none of my knowledge or dedication mattered to the community, because I was "just" a girl.

In many ways, our religion did not take women seriously. And in many ways, women returned the favor. "The ladies" showed up only on the big holidays and at the tail end of Sabbath services (if at all), and they talked incessantly after arriving. I constantly had to strain my eyes and ears to focus on the services. When I sang, my voice seldom blended with the voices from behind, for the women's section usually was devoid of prayer. As such, it just never seemed the place to turn for preserving our traditions.

This year, I sucked in my breath in anticipation. The congregation started off by singing a few Mizrahi songs, but within minutes we were bowled over by Ashkenazi-Israeli songs belted out once again by the new rabbi and his two cohorts.

I absolutely *had* to stop the insanity, and I knew from the last two years that I could not do it alone. For the first time in my life, I stopped facing forward and turned to look behind me.

I was stunned. I suddenly realized the latent potential that had been there all along. I jumped out of my seat and began marching up and down the aisle of the crowded section, clapping and singing at the top of my lungs, rousing all the women into rowdy Mizrahi song: *"Simhoona, simhoona besimhath hatorah . . ."*

I chose songs that were easy to follow, with repetitive phrases, and all the women jumped right in, expressions snapping from boredom into glee. As the women's section began drowning out the Ashkenazi songs, the passive men woke up and joined in with us. Pretty soon, we had taken over the whole synagogue with Mizrahi songs.

The young rabbi started getting agitated. He wanted control. I marched up from the women's section, crossed into the men's, climbed the steps onto the *teba*—the rabbi's platform—and yelled at him, "There are at least *ten* Ashkenazi synagogues down this street alone. If you want to sing Ashkenazi songs, then go to one of those synagogues. But don't you *dare* try to bring those songs in here. This is an *Iraqi* synagogue, and it's the only one we have!" With that, I marched back down the steps and into the women's section.

All hell broke loose. Everyone started yelling at one another. I had brought to the surface tensions that had been growing over the past few years: What direction would the synagogue go in? Would it "adapt" (assimilate) to the "modern" (Ashkenazi) ways, or would it stay pure? There was a definite split in the congregation.

In my experience, Iraqi Jews cannot stand unpleasantness, and they will bend over backward to avoid it. This situation was no exception. After arguments ensued, the young rabbi and his two cohorts began gathering people into the room off to the side of the sanctuary, and people just followed. The three traitors got everyone into the side room to dance around with the Torah, the Hebrew bible—which is strictly forbidden by Iraqi practice— while singing Ashkenazi-Israeli songs like "Hava Nagila."

The resisters went home.

I remember seeing one of my favorite old men dancing around with the crowd, gathering people together, trying to make everyone forget they had just fought. I was shocked to see him actively participating in the erasure of our tradition.

Walking with my family through the hullabaloo, I had a sinking feeling. People were dancing, but it felt like death. As we neared the exit, I knew the resisters had lost and my family probably would not return. We pushed open the door and walked out as a boy younger than I shouted, "And don't come back!" *Slam.* He shut the door. I started to cry.

Eight years later, I moved to Los Angeles. I avoided that synagogue, not looking forward to how congregants, especially the rabbi, would respond to me. When I finally visited, I realized I had given far too much credit to their consciousness. Unable to fathom that a girl could be the source of such commotion, the few men who mentioned the situation seemed to think my *father* was the one who had raised the ruckus, not me.

Offended yet relieved, I did not bother correcting them.

loolwa khazzoom (www.loolwa.com) graduated Phi Beta Kappa from Troublemakers "R" Us. She is the author of *Consequence: Beyond Resisting Rape* (Pearl in a Million Press), editor of *Behind the Veil of Silence: Middle Eastern and North African Jewish Women Speak Out*, and coordinator of the Jewish Multicultural Curriculum Project. Since yelling at the rabbi, she went on to create the first-ever egalitarian Mizrahi services. This essay was first published in *Generation J*–www.generationj.com.

Diary of an Urban Guerilla
kathy bruin

8:00 A.M. We're postering the city tonight and it's raining buckets. The forecast says seventy-mile-per-hour winds and "one hundred percent chance of rain in all areas all day." Great.

I have long been frustrated with the way women are depicted in our culture—the emphasis is always on looks over brains or talent. My frustration heightened in 1995 when I overheard a mother offering her preteen daughter a cookie. The girl took it, saying, "Sure; I can start my diet *tomorrow.*" I was surprised. "It's starting so young," I thought, making the link between the depiction of females in the media and the stories I'd read about girls' self-esteem plummeting around age twelve. Images of women in popular culture (led by advertising, entertainment, and "beauty" industries) affect girls' perceptions of themselves and encourage eating disorders. Every year billions of dollars are spent on advertising; every day we see hundreds of glossy images. This barrage is effective. It is virtually impossible to keep from internalizing these industries' beauty standards, and difficult to offer criticism or alternative images that can have a real impact—unless you have the money to buy your own billboards. Or an inclination to become an Urban Guerilla.

Not long after the cookie incident, I became obsessed with Obsession. Calvin Klein's perfume ads had been around for years, but an especially annoying new one sent me over the edge. On municipal buses and huge billboards towering over the city, Kate Moss reclined nude, her bones so accentuated and her face so sunken, she looked as if she was starving. *Why isn't anybody mad about this?* I wondered. I sure was. I wanted to do something, something louder than writing Calvin Klein a letter. I knew others also had to be sick of seeing models photographed to look as scrawny, weak, and vulnerable as possible. I wanted to do something big enough so that others might be motivated to do something as well. At first I envisioned myself scrambling up the scaffolding to deface the billboards. But instead, I chased after buses for weeks until I got a good photo of the ad. Then I scanned it into a computer and changed the text to read: "Emaciation Stinks—Stop Starvation Imagery." I made posters and conned friends and family into helping me plaster the city. About-Face, a San Francisco group dedicated to combating negative images of women, was born.

3:30 P.M. I have such a nervous stomach. I am always nervous on poster nights, but this torrential downpour is making me crazy. I fear volunteers are already jumping ship and making other plans. I've got to try and eat something.

My goal in using posters is to make a public statement that is familiar: stylish, big, and on the streets with the other images. Our second poster was of a brightly colored circus cage (like on a box of animal crackers) with fashion models trapped inside. The banner read, "Please Don't Feed the Models." The cage was a perfect symbol of the ways women are kept—and keep themselves—in check, not only by the beauty rituals that hold us captive (not leaving the house without makeup, not going to the beach with hairy legs), but also by the constant pressure to remain within verbal, physical, and sexual confines. I scrawled the idea on a napkin one night, gave it to my graphic artists, and two weeks later pasted the big posters all over the city in honor of National Eating Disorders Awareness Week.

7:00 P.M. We decide to go ahead despite the rain. Twenty-three people show up. We divide into nine teams, each with paste, rollers, and a map with a specific section of the city circled. It is still drizzling as we set out.

Postering is thrilling. It's rebellious, and you envision yourself skulking in the streets looking shiftily back and forth like a spy. It's a rare event that brings kidlike excitement to a bunch of cynical city dwellers, and the combination of doing something that's illegal *and* that you feel strongly about is too compelling to resist. It makes you feel powerful and righteous; it makes you think you can effect real change in the world.

On the downside, I have been tracked down and screamed at by construction managers, causing my stomach to knot. I am a hyperresponsible person, the classic "good girl." Yet I do what I think is right in my gut even if I might get in trouble or piss someone off. We don't set out to anger construction managers or create more work for them, but guerilla tactics are a perfect way to reach people on the same visual level that billboards do. And they get media attention. The week I posted my Obsession spoof I appeared on five television newscasts and countless newspaper and radio programs. Since our first postering, About-Face has received support from thousands around the world. Phone messages, letters, and e-mails come from parents, teachers, school nurses, grandmothers, and teenage girls themselves. They say, "Thank goodness someone is taking this on." They say, "How can we help?"

9:00 P.M. The teams come back with paste in their hair and on their clothes, and with stories to tell: "We totally plastered this site near the park." "People were stopping and asking about the posters, so we gave them some." "We ran out of paste and bought flour to make more."

We collect the goopy rollers, rags, and cans, load up the cars, hug, and say "See you next time." My volunteers are ordinary, law-abiding, polite types who go home gushing with bravado. They, like me, are transformed by the experience.

The day after a postering, many of the 400+ posters will be torn down by annoyed construction workers. But some will stay up for months. While they won't be as noticed as a Calvin Klein billboard, they will still produce a reaction. Some folks will miss the point, others will totally get it, and some—like you?—may even be inspired to perpetrate an urban assault of your own. After that, you may find yourself on a cross-town bus, passing a poster hung on a plywood wall. A sense of pride will well up in you. You'll smile smugly and turn to the stranger next to you: "I did that," you'll brag. And you should; instead of being complacent, you took a stand.

kathy bruin (www.about-face.org), who lives in San Francisco, wonders if she can keep her day job if she gets arrested. To make your own wheat paste, mix three tablespoons of flour with a small amount of cold water. Add one cup of hot water. Bring to a boil, stirring constantly, until mixture thickens. Cool and enjoy. A version of this essay first appeared in *Bitch* magazine.

∽

Next are two girls-in-pants stories: one kinda quiet, one kinda not. Interestingly enough, they happened at the same time but in different places. Girl telepathy? –Rivka

Civil Disobedience: A Primary School Primer
debra kolodny

Girls were not allowed to wear pants in my elementary school. This was PS 104, a public school, so no uniform was involved.

The rationale was pure gender stereotyping; pants were simply considered inappropriate attire for girls in the late 1960s.

One freezing winter day when I was eight and in the third grade, I decided that common sense should prevail over this rule. I don't think I struggled long with this decision, but I'm sure I conferred with my mother. After checking the outdoor thermometer and seeing its bitter cold reading, she was with me. So I pulled on a pair of pants, grabbed my brown-bag lunch, and headed out, braced for both the weather and the angry lecture I expected to get at school.

As usual, I walked around the corner and three houses down to pick up my friend Mindy so we could walk together. When she opened the front door, Mindy saw my pants. She was wearing a skirt. As soon as we got outside, she changed her mind. We went back in and she put on pants. The two of us went to school that day warm, comfortable, and betrousered. Our teacher didn't say a word. Nobody told us not to do it again. I took that as a positive sign, and I didn't wear a skirt again for three years.

I guess I was an elementary-school role model, because soon after that day, other girls started wearing pants, too. The clothing barrier had been broken forever at PS 104. I didn't get an award at assembly for this—in fact, no one ever mentioned it—but in my heart I felt like a champion.

debra kolodny grew from a barrier-breaking baby feminist into a barrier-breaking adult feminist. A social-justice lefty who leads services at her *chavura* (Jewish community), she wears whatever makes her comfortable, pants or skirt, usually purple or fuchsia (since you asked). Find Debra's book, *Blessed Bi Spirit: Bisexual People of Faith* (Continuum-International Press), at www.geocities.com/rosefirerising/blest.

∞

Nine Days to Change the World

terri m. muehe

DAY 1, SUNDAY: THE IDEA

"I'm tired of freezing my ass off every morning waiting for the school bus," my friend Roberta said as we lay on her bed eating Fritos out of the bag.

"It's such a dumb rule," Eda scowled.

I nodded in agreement. "Yeah, we should do something about it."

Eda, Roberta, and I were best friends in the seventh grade at Junior High West, a 2,400-student school in a suburb outside of Boston. It was early winter, in the late 1960s, and microminis—very, very short skirts—were "in." Pantyhose hadn't made it to the mass market yet, so we actually had to wear stockings and garter belts, which I *hated*. The garters/short skirt combination made it difficult to even move without revealing too much. However, at the time, every school in the country had a dress code. Skirts were the only option for girls, even during the coldest winter months.

"Hey, wait. I have an idea," I said, grabbing the last handful of Fritos. "Tomorrow, just for one day, let's wear pants to school to protest."

I may have been a little shrimp—I weighed only sixty-nine pounds—but I had a strong social conscience. It was during the height of what they called "the Vietnamese conflict," and I regularly skipped school to go to all kinds of protests: Stop the War, Ban the Bomb, End World Hunger, Fight for Women's Lib. Though only eleven and twelve years old, all of my friends were politically active. We had politics before we had our periods. ✳

DAY 2, MONDAY: PLANTING THE SEED

Eda, Roberta, and I hid our pants in our book bags so our mothers wouldn't see them, then we changed in the girls' room before the first bell. We were excited. The stir began as soon we left the bathroom. A buzz just started. You have to understand, today it would be like someone walking buck-naked down the hallway. We weren't in pants long—fifteen minutes tops—before the homeroom teacher sent us to the principal's office.

"Do you want me to call your parents?" Principal Harry was a typical authority-figure-macho-schmuck. He tried to bully us. "This is the school rule . . . *blah, blah, blah.*"

We had expected this. We knew we'd be forced to change; being rebels, we just wanted to see how long it would take. Even after we were back in our miniskirts, word spread. It was *the* subject of conversation during all three lunch periods. Some girls even talked about bringing pants the next day: "Right on. Maybe *I'll* do it tomorrow."

DAY 3, TUESDAY: PICKING UP SPEED

Sure enough, we got to school and it was like a dressing room changing party in the girls' lavatory. Soon there were several dozen of us wearing pants.

"Any girls wearing pants, please put skirts on immediately or you will be sent home. Your parents will be called . . . *blah, blah, blah,*" the principal said over the loudspeaker during homeroom. A foolish move on his part: Anyone who hadn't yet heard about the revolt sure did then.

As instructed, we filed out of homeroom, and had a second party in the girls' bathroom.

DAY 4, WEDNESDAY: STRENGTH IN NUMBERS

Probably two hundred girls crammed into the bathrooms to change that morning. Some even came to school wearing pants (it *was* winter, after all). I don't remember being forced back into skirts that third day of the rebellion. *This is great,* I thought. *Maybe something can really change here.*

DAY 5, THURSDAY: CAN'T STOP A MOVING TRAIN

Who knows how many girls wore pants that day; at least several hundred.

I'm not sure who came up with the idea—me, Eda, or Roberta—but at lunchtime we started spreading the word down the long tables that we were going to stage a walkout the next day and hold a sit-down strike in the parking lot! *"Psst.* The dress code has got to go. Pass it on."

Word spread quickly. Some kids just liked the idea of getting out of classes for an hour, but a core group of us looked at this from a purely political point of view. Equal rights for girls were important to us. Only this time we wouldn't have to skip school to attend the protest.

What we didn't know was that news of our plan had spread to Harry—and beyond.

DAY 6, FRIDAY: RESISTANCE

We arrived to find stern-looking adults stationed up and down the corridors at regular intervals on each of the four floors of our school. (Today, over thirty years later, I can't recall exactly who those adults were. Perhaps teachers. Maybe parents. My usually crystal-clear memory wants to say it was the *cops.* Could it have been?) *"Oh my god,"* I whispered to Roberta. "They're taking us seriously." I was completely shocked, but, like others, undeterred.

The set time for the walkout neared. It was a cold day, cold enough that we could not just leave without getting our coats . . . from our lockers . . . where the authoritative adults were posted. We prepared to move toward those lockers when suddenly Curmudgeon Harry's voice crackled over the loudspeaker: "Anyone caught leaving school will be suspended." (Not that that would have stopped Eda and me.) "This will not happen," he continued, "you are not going to walk out . . . *blah, blah, blah."* Then he added, "We will be holding both PTA and school board meetings over the weekend to reexamine the issue of the school dress code."

Eda, Roberta, and I smiled at one another across the classroom. *We'd done it.*

The walkout never happened. It didn't need to.

DAY 7, SATURDAY: THE POWER OF THE PRESS

It made the papers. A junior high school filled with more than two thousand eleven-, twelve-, and thirteen-year-olds about to hold a walkout? How could it not?

DAY 8, SUNDAY: CAPITULATION

It was in the papers again. This time the article said the school board had met and the dress code rule mandating girls wear skirts had been officially abolished.

DAY 9, MONDAY: VICTORY

We showed up Monday and that was it. The entire school was in pants. We had taken a stand and made a change.

FOREVER AFTER

Shortly after our town's "skirts-only" rule was abolished, the Greater Boston School District dismantled theirs. Then New York City did, too. Then Los Angeles. I don't know if our actions, and people reading about them in the newspapers, caused this, or if other people were taking similar steps simultaneously, but in the absence of anyone's telling me otherwise, I feel okay saying *we'd wanted to make a change for a day and we made a change for a country*. All before our first periods.

terri m. muehe (DOLPHIN7XS@aol.com) is an artist and an advocate serving on the Board of Directors of a New Hampshire coalition of AIDS Service Organizations. To this day, she hates stockings and pantyhose. And although she does own skirts and dresses, she only wears them "under protest."

∞

Women's Rights Are Human Rights

rana husseini

When a murder occurs in Jordan, they do not give out the victim's name or address. So when I walked through a poor and crowded suburb outside our capital, Amman, navigating sandy, hilly, unpaved roads, I was not exactly sure where I'd end up. Figuring everyone knew everyone's business in this neighborhood, I stopped an older man on the street.

"I heard there was a crime here. A sixteen-year-old girl was killed by her oldest brother. Can you tell me the address?"

"Right there." He pointed behind me to a barbershop.

"Do you know why she was killed?" I asked.

"Because her other brother had raped her."

"You must be joking."

"No."

"Are you sure?"

"Yes." He nodded his head, offering no look of shock to match mine.

"There must be something wrong."

"No, that's what happened."

It was an old barbershop with two chairs. The barber sat on one; two men stood nearby. I walked in, angry but cautious, and without delay asked about the girl.

"Who told you? How do you know about this?" the men responded in a *how-dare-you-ask* tone.

"It was in the newspaper. Just a few lines," I answered.

When they said they were her uncles, I sat down, told them I was a reporter, and launched in: "Why was she killed?"

"She was not a good girl," one uncle snapped, as if that would justify a killing.

But I knew the truth from the man in the street. Now I wanted it from them. I pushed with more questions. Finally, one decided there was no reason to hide the truth: "Her brother raped her."

That was all I needed to hear. "So why did you kill *her*? Why did you punish the victim? Why didn't you punish the brother?"

To those outside our culture my questions may have seemed presumptuous. But by then I understood enough about so-called "honor crimes" to know that though the uncles hadn't actually slit her throat (her oldest brother had done that), they had *plotted* the execution. That is how it is usually done: by family decision. Now, much to their repugnance, a *woman* was asking about this crime of honor.

The uncles looked at each other, haughtily amused by my questions. One asked the other, "Do you think we killed the wrong person?"

"No, no, relax; we killed the right one."

These are words I will never forget: words that still make my blood burn.

"She seduced her brother. She tarnished the family's honor and deserved to die. That is why we killed her."

"Why would she seduce her *brother* when there are dozens of men on the street?" I openly argued with them.

Fed up with me, and turning more aggressive, they shot back: "Why are you here, why do you care? Why aren't you dressed in the traditional robe? Why aren't you married? Oh, you studied in the United States?" These accusations, fired like bullets, translated to one thing: Like their niece, I was not a good girl.

Indeed I *had* worn nontraditional clothes—jeans and sneakers—on this murder investigation, just in case something went wrong and I had to take off fast. I figured now was a good time to leave. Anyway, I already had my story.

In 1994, when I was twenty-six and investigating this girl's death for my newspaper, the *Jordan Times,* I never imagined her sad story would instigate my becoming a national voice for the mostly poor victims of so-called honor killings. What is a crime of honor? It is when a male takes the life of his female relative because, in the family's opinion, she has tarnished their reputation by supposedly getting involved in "immoral behaviors."

Though honor killings are a violation of human rights and a violation of all major faiths, including Jordan's predominant Islamic religion, many Arab people ignore the killings and pretend they do not exist. Or they justify the act, as one killer did with me: "This is our culture. If I did not do it, I would shame my family. Blood cleanses honor."

Sometime after that disturbing incident at the barbershop, I went to the courthouse to investigate further. I sifted through legal paperwork and testimonies to understand the case's circumstances, the victim, and the suspect. Then I rushed to my newspaper with all these facts circulating in my mind. Trying to be objective and at the same time exposing the brutality and unjust sentencing, I wrote my second-ever news report on honor killings.

I learned astonishing things investigating those early articles, such as that women are often killed under the pretense of honor, when in reality their families murder them because of baseless rumors, suspicion, incest they want to hide, inheritance manipulation, or simply because females are considered a burden on families. I learned that even though premeditated murder is usually punished by life in prison or death, due to Jordan's laws some honor-crime killers get only two- to seven-year sentences. Many get even more shockingly short sentences—*three to six months!* Another discovery I made was that women who are under threat of, or those who survive, a murder attempt by their families for "immoral behaviors" are themselves indefinitely imprisoned by the authorities, ostensibly for protection. However, a woman cannot *choose* to leave prison, nor bail herself out. And if her family bails her out, it is likely because they plan to kill her. I have met women who have been locked up for eight years, with no end in sight. Everywhere else in the world the *aggressor* is put behind bars, not the victim.

I was angered and distressed: Women-killers were getting away with murder, and women's human rights were being ignored. I decided to expose these injustices through my articles. I hoped that one day someone would hear me and be just as enraged.

I was heard, all right. Since my first of many news reports on this taboo topic, the newspaper has received numerous supportive letters. Then, as time passed, as the issue (and e-mail) became more prominent in Jordan, the negative comments started coming in. They questioned my motives. "Why are you reporting on honor killings?" they asked. "You are . . ."

"encouraging sexual freedom and promiscuity among women."

"backed by the West, and aiming to destroy the morals of our people."

"imposing Western values on our conservative society."

"tarnishing the country's image by exposing our dirty laundry abroad."

And my favorite: "a radical feminist, seeking fame through these news reports."

One high-up official, a woman, yelled at my editor: "You should stop Rana Husseini. She is exaggerating. These things do not happen here!"

As before, these words became fire burning inside me. Instead of making me stop, they kept me going. I was determined to prove the killings happened, even in the face of anonymous e-mail threats, such as "Stop writing about this issue or you will be 'visited' by someone at your work or home."

I am not scared. I know what I am doing is right, and when you fight for something that's right, you shouldn't be scared. I know the people and the government must be held accountable for these women's deaths. All should bear the responsibility of ensuring women's safety and their right to life.

I have argued this point with judges—carefully, of course. The judiciary is one of the most respected institutions in our country. You can't really question or accuse them of anything. But when a man who had killed his sister (because she was raped) received a six month sentence for this premeditated murder, I knocked on the office door of a judge from the trial and we calmly "chatted" off the record. The judge knew me and had seen me on TV, fighting for women's rights.

"Why did you give that murderer such a lenient sentence? The girl was raped. It's not her fault."

"The defendant is a product of our culture. He was pressured by society and his family to take such actions."

Clearly, the light punishment showed the defendant was not the only one who was a product of our culture. "There is something wrong here," I told the judge. "These verdicts do not value women's lives."

He paused. I could see the conversation had an impact.

Now, the impact I see is nationwide. The personal accusations have not stopped, but in the past seven years of my reporting, lecturing, speaking on local, national, and international TV, appearing in documentaries worldwide, winning human rights awards, and earning international recognition, I have also seen real change. A group of us formed a grassroots organization, the National Jordanian Campaign to Eliminate so-called Crimes of Honor. We collected an unprecedented fifteen thousand signatures, calling for the abolishment of specific laws that discriminate against women, and presented them to decision makers and the Parliament. We also held Jordan's first march for women's rights, and five thousand people came. With the support of the royal family, there is now a growing movement demanding a guarantee of justice, freedom, and the right to life for women in my country.

rana husseini (ranahuss@nets.com.jo) continues her work as a journalist focusing on honor crimes for the *Jordan Times.* In 1998 she won the Reebok Human Rights Award, and in 2000 her organization was recognized with the Human Rights Watch Monitor's Award. Back in her college days in the United States, Rana was captain of the women's basketball team, and she still likes to wear sneakers.

CHAPTER 7

"That's Not Nice!": Acting On Anger

BRAZEN BABES IN COMBAT BOOTS

STEPPING OUT OF LINE

Being cheeky by not turning the other cheek

Women, Niceness, and Anger Myth One: Anger is unladylike. (Like *ladies* don't get pissed off, too? What about when our tea gets cold?) Myth Two: Women are nice, nurturing caregivers. (Well, yes. All the time? Hardly—and if so, perhaps to our detriment.)

Feeling angry is a healthy human response to being hurt. Whether one person disrespects a girl, or lots of people build institutions that leave her out, she is justified in being mad. No hesitation, no apology necessary. Part of what makes a person whole is the ability to *express* anger. It is natural to pound a fist on the table every once in a while. Expressing anger keeps a woman from turning it inward—a contributor to depression.

But the Be Nice, Dear finishing school many attend—simply by growing up in our society—trains girls to not show anger. (Kind of like how the Be Strong, Son prep school trains boys to not show sadness.) The school's rules are unrelenting. Take Number 752: *Being nice means being accommodating.* (After a few years of that, a girl might need re-educating to simply learn how to say *no.*) Girls are taught to be understanding, to make room for why someone may act inappropriately. When a man "acts out" (warning: euphemism for *harasses*), a girl is to sit quiet, let it go, just take it. Here's the distinction they forgot at finishing school: Being nice is a good thing. Being nice *all the time* can keep a girl complacent.

"The first thing they taught in my self-defense class," one chapter contributor told me, "is that before we can defend ourselves, we have to give ourselves permission to *not be nice.*"

What? You mean saying *please* won't stop a rapist?

Like a mama bear defending her cubs, women defend their babies. So why don't more fight back in defense of themselves? Women are smart. They can assess when talking or fighting back will be too risky. But when it's worth the risk, what's the hesitation then? Self-defense is innately human; could it have been conditioned out of women to protect themselves? Rule Number 3,004: *Don't hit back.* It is considered stepping out of Girlie Line even if a woman *responds* to violence someone else started.

The question is, when does it make sense to shrug off this conditioning? When is it justified to yell, hit back, retaliate, match the level of violence the assailant already started? When is it escalating the violence and when is it self-defense, or the firing of a warning shot that says, "Stop—or else!"? Right now, abusive men know: It's a safe bet when you target a woman that you won't have a fight on your hands. That's why women are targeted so much more than men. If there were consequences for inappropriate or violent behavior (that is, if women verbally or physically fought back), would abusive men be less apt to target women?

Anger is tricky. A woman needs to decide when and with whom it should be expressed. If she wants to "reach" someone, have them understand how their behavior hurt her, if she wants to change their heart and mind, anger may not be a useful tool. It may trigger their defense mechanisms and keep them from being able to hear her. But sometimes a girl isn't trying to "reach" a perpetrator or someone who mistreats her. Sometimes a girl just wants to fight back or make the statement, *This behavior has got to stop!*

This chapter is full of women who choose to act on, instead of swallow, their anger. They are not settling a conflict with nice talk, compassion, or understanding. Some stories are about self-defense; most are about retaliation for being wronged. Some may go over the line of what is generally considered acceptable or principled behavior—perhaps readers will see them as overreactions to originally justifiable anger. But these are real women in the real world. Their acts are not prettied up for our benefit. These women have just had it. Fed up, they refuse to be used or abused another minute without taking a stand.

The main message in this most controversial chapter is: It is liberating to know that females can express anger. Thinking that they must always be nice keeps them accepting abuse way longer than they should. Keeps them from fighting back when it makes sense to fight back. If women and girls know they don't have to be nice all the time, then they will not hesitate to stand up for themselves when mistreated or to fight back if attacked.

How to Stop a Thief

mary going

Working the night shift at a truck stop in rural Maine meant I served "breakfast" to all the drunks who came in after the bars closed. On this particular night, my section was packed. I didn't have time to clear a table before the next set of customers sat down.

At one point, two men came in and sat at a table where some of my regular customers had just been. The regulars always tipped me well, but on this night, after the men sat down, there was nothing. I was pretty sure the two guys had stolen the money, but I wasn't positive until I was out of their sight behind the coffee machine and overheard one (the instigator) tell his buddy that he should get the money off the next table, too.

I knew what I had to do. I filled a pitcher to the top with ice water and went to their table. I was nervous, but as I poured the jerk's glass full, I "accidentally" dumped the entire pitcher of freezing water into his lap. As he stood up in shock, I got right in his face and told him that if he ever stole money from me again, it would be "f***ing hot coffee."

Swimming in water, he paid for his untouched meal and didn't complain to management. As you can imagine, they found out anyway and fired me. Let me assure you, *it was worth it.*

mary going lives in Maine, manages a superhero website about hot sauce (www.firegirl.com), and in general does not have a particular fondness for ice water.

∞

Eye on the Ball
kathleen antonia

Plain-looking and out of touch with the latest fads, I wasn't popular with the girls at my high school. I probably would have cared more about their rejection if I hadn't had The Boys. The Boys were my everything. They asked me how I was doing and cared about the answer. They were impressed with my smarts and complimented me when I actually managed an outfit not too far out of fashion. We teased each other, supported each other, and helped each other kick major butt on the athletic field. That was why they liked me. At seventeen years old, I benched more than 90 percent of the guys on the varsity football team. Unfortunately, I did not attend a school that allowed girls to play tackle football. But The Boys knew my skills. I taught them a thing or two, and they smiled when they saw me in the hall: an even trade. The girls didn't get it. They figured there could be no possible reason to justify my popularity with the members of the football team, except that I must be sleeping around. In fact, I was a virgin, and I planned on keeping it that way.

One evening after practice (track and field for me, football for them), I drove three of the team's finest to their respective homes. One, Alexi, demanded he sit shotgun. As I rounded a dark street corner toward his family's apartment, he ran his fingers up my inner thigh and with his other hand tried to grab my right breast. Alexi was my friend, so I was more pissed off than scared. Mostly I was trying to figure out how to get out of this situation. I pushed his hands away, downshifted, and steered around the corner all at the same time (a feat of which I am particularly proud). The two in the backseat laughed. Encouraged, Alexi tried again. I again pushed his hands away, finally stopping the car.

"Get out, all of you."

The two in the backseat were quick to exit. Alexi remained shotgun and turned toward me. Leaning in for a kiss, he whispered, "You know you want me."

Others surely would have; after all, he was the star of the football team. And I did consider it, for a second. I looked at his soft, pouting lips, his dark eyes, his nearing, muscular body. I imagined what it would feel like to have his mouth upon mine, his hands roaming all over me.

Nope, I decided. *Not today, and certainly not this way.*

"Get out," I demanded. I had said that before, however, and it hadn't worked. This time, to make my point perfectly clear, I went for the only vulnerable spot on his impervious body: I grabbed the crotch of his pants and squeezed lightly.

"Let go, Kathleen," he ordered, clearly shocked.

"Unlock the door," I growled. I was not going to let go, I told myself, no matter what might happen.

"Let go, first!" Alexi commanded. But as I squeezed tighter, he gingerly released the lock.

"Now open the door."

Alexi complied and asked, "Are you going to let go now?"

"Get out," I seethed. Still holding onto his package, stretching my long arm across the passenger seat, I guided him out of my car and into a stagnant puddle near the curb. "Now lock the door, and close it."

"You're still holding onto me," he whimpered.

"Lock the door."

Alexi looked sheepishly into my burning face, his pitiful round eyes stained red with tears. There he was, the delight of high-school football fans across the state, looking ready to collapse.

"On the count of three, you're going to push the door closed," I said. "And on the count of three-and-a-half, I'm going to let go. Ready?"

"Wait, wait, wait!" Alexi pleaded.

"One, one-and-a-half, two, two-and-a-half, three."

Alexi pushed the door to swing it closed. At the same time, I let go and drove off. *Three-and-a-half, four.* I felt relieved. I also felt sad. After all, this was a friend I had trusted.

I never drove any of The Boys home again. The girls at school were certain I must have taken a vow of celibacy. In fact, they were sort of right. Determined that it would happen on my terms, and with the right person, I remained a virgin until long after graduation.

kathleen antonia :(FanMail@tweaked.net) is an X-generation singer/acter (yes, with an "e"—to make the word gender neutral). She has performed onstage with the California African-American Shakespeare Company and at the Annual San Francisco HIV Prevention Awards. And since we know you want to know, Antonia chucked her virginity after high school when she found a fellow footballer who was the right person and who did it on her terms.

∞

Mike Meets the Dykes
judith k. witherow

We had just finished eating dinner when the first call came. It was my younger sister. She usually kept her life private, but this night she was asking for help in whispered tones. Before she could finish saying what was going on, I heard her boyfriend, Mike, demand she hang up. After the call, Sue and I discussed whether to go to her apartment or just wait. Mike had a drinking problem, and like many others with his addiction, he became abusive after enough alcohol coated his cowardice. The phone rang again. More whispering: not because Mike might overhear, but because he had choked her, damaging her vocal cords. Her three youngest children were crying in the background.

"Barricade the apartment door. Don't let him back in. We're on our way," I said.

Sue and I drove to my sister's apartment, where we saw a struggle had taken place. Her always immaculate home looked like a hurricane had touched down.

"Where are the children?" I asked.

Three little heads came up from behind the overturned couch where they were hiding. "Hi, Aunt Judy. Hi, Aunt Sue," they said. The relief on their faces fueled our rage.

"Where's Mike?" I was boiling now. *This had gone on long enough.*

"Probably at one of the bars," Sis said.

We nodded and handed her a baseball bat for protection.

Sue and I started cruising the parking lots of neighborhood dives. We discussed possible ways to confront Mike to stop this madness, but dealing with an alcoholic rarely allows reason as an option. We came to the conclusion that we'd have to be prepared for anything. As someone who came from generations of alcoholics, I knew violence was only one swig of liquor away.

At the second bar, we spotted Mike's pickup truck. Adrenaline began seeping from my every pore. We discussed disabling his vehicle so he couldn't leave before we "chatted him up." Our first idea was to remove the distributor cap. No good: the hood was chained and padlocked. (What does that tell you about Mike?) Plan B: Flatten a tire.

"Do you have your pocketknife?" Sue asked, rhetorically.

My knife is like the credit card in that commercial; I don't leave home without it. She leaned down and stuck the blade in up to the handle. I didn't know if the tire would explode or what, but it went so smoothly, we decided to puncture another.

"I'm cutting the tires high up on the whitewall, so they can't be fixed," Sue explained.

Nice touch. *How do I love thee, my woman? Let me count the ways . . .*

Next, we peered inside the bar's glass front door and immediately saw Mike in the foyer talking on the pay phone. When Sue pulled the door open, we heard him yelling at my sister. He was threatening to hurt her and the children again!

From there on it was like watching a surreal movie. Sue looked as if she was walking in slow motion as she crossed the floor in three long strides. Her arms lifted up and she wrapped both hands around Mike's throat. The phone receiver dropped and swung back and forth like a pendulum. Without loosening her grip on his neck, Sue began beating his head against the plate-glass window. With each slam she said, "How do *you* like it? How do *you* like it?" His tongue had little trouble touching the bottom of his chin. His eyes looked like twin eight balls racked—and still she didn't stop. In all our years together, I'd never seen her like this.

God, she's gonna kill him, I thought.

My plan of staying outside ended. I couldn't allow her to get into trouble because of him.

When I loosened her hold, he was barely able to stand. He wobbled around, feeling for a bar stool to sit on. As if nothing was happening, his compadres continued their drinking. The woman tending bar, on the other hand, came out yelling, "I called the police!" I told her what had inspired the incident, but she didn't care. "Out. Now." She pointed to the door.

The pause gave Mike enough time to catch his breath and

regain his boozy bravado. He started making threats. He had nearly been killed, and yet he still acted as if he had won.

Without thinking, I walked over and stuck my forefinger in under his sternum. "Your days of tormenting my sister and her children are over. I'm going to cut your f***ing heart out."

The way his face froze, he must have thought my finger was my knife. Maybe the bartender did, too. She kept yelling, "The police are on their way! The police are on their way!"

And they were; we heard the faint wail of sirens. "Time to go," I said. We exited the bar and ran to our car. As we pulled out, the police pulled in—parking in the same spot we had vacated. They must have seen us leaving and not given it a second thought: *Two women. Nothing important. Gotta hurry and stop the bullies beating up the guy inside.*

Later that night, while we were reviewing the bar scene with my sister, Mike called.

"Come pack up your crap and vacate the apartment," I told him. He did.

Unfortunately, that wasn't the end of Mike. He made another appearance six months later, insisting on moving back in. Sis simply had to pick up the phone, and Sue and I arrived within minutes. Once again, we escorted him and his belongings outside. As I stood in the open doorway to make sure he left, he swaggered to his truck, pulled a .12-gauge shotgun out of the gun rack, and laid it on the seat. Was it meant for my sister, or for me? It didn't matter. I stood my ground, figuring if necessary I'd fall backward into the apartment before he could get a shot off. Luckily for all of us, Mike just left and never came back. He finally understood: The Dyke Disposal Unit (DDU) need only hear the plea of a woman in trouble before they'd be there on the double.

judith k. witherow (jwandsl@aol.com) is a Native American lesbian-feminist writer and storyteller, and winner of the 1994 Audre

Lorde Memorial Prose contest. She is also cofounder/president of DDU, which has chapters in all states nationwide. Join today!

∞

Charmed, I'm Sure
audrey schaefer

I was at a restaurant bar with two girlfriends when a man approached us. It took only three seconds before he started acting like a jerk. When he then asked if he could buy me a drink, I said, "No, but could I have the money instead?"

That did the trick; he fled quickly.

audrey schaefer (schaefer@schaefer.com) continues to fine-tune her tactfulness in Maryland. This story took place when she was in college, and she now runs her own business—a public relations agency.

∞

Closing the Nasty Girl
elizabeth o'neill

Women lazed across multicolored blankets dotting the grass, passing jugs of Kool-Aid and listening to the band play "Girls Just Want to Have Fun." I had expected frightened, upset people, but this looked like a summer camp sleepover.

I glanced sideways at my boyfriend, Kevin (who was discreetly checking out other women), before spotting Stella under the *Mad-at-Dad* banner. "Seen anyone from group?" I asked her. The night before we'd tried to talk members of our incest survivors' support group into coming to this Father's Day rally.

"No, just us."

A middle-aged woman took the podium. She began reading the names of women and girls killed by husbands, boyfriends, and fathers. *Mary Jane Doe: Ex-husband stalked her for six months before shooting her outside the Laundromat. Lucy Jane Doe: Boyfriend beat her to death after burning his mouth on the dinner she'd served him. Baby Jane Doe: Father slammed her head against the rails of her crib, dead before she even had a name.* Nancy Jane Doe. Sally Jane Doe. The list went on.

"I have to go meet Judy," Kevin announced suddenly. Judy was Kevin's old girlfriend. He was seeing more of her lately.

"Okay then," I said, too quickly. "See you later."

"Do you suppose he's screwing her?" Stella asked after he was out of earshot.

I hesitated, ran my hand over the grass. "Yeah, I suppose so."

Women lined up at the gazebo. One by one, they walked to the microphone to broadcast the names of men who had violated them, sometimes saying what the men did. As Stella and I took our places in line, a large brick lay heavy in my stomach.

"You didn't do anything wrong," Stella whispered. *"They* did."

I went first, reciting the names. *My father—molested me. My brother—molested me. My therapist—molested me.* I was sick of protecting them and not myself. Then it was Stella's turn. She reached for my hand. *My brother—molested me. My teacher—molested me.*

My legs wobbled as we walked from the podium. The line of incest survivors stretched around the gazebo, twice. After we sat back down, two women moved from blanket to blanket spreading the word. "Stick around after the rally," they whispered. "We're planning an action."

Fifteen minutes later, a small crowd gathered behind the gazebo. "Okay, listen up," said a short, muscular woman, with curly blond hair. She looked like a high-school basketball coach, without the whistle. "We're marching to the Red Light District to occupy one of the porn shops."

I felt my face turn red. My father had brought me to the District when I was fifteen. I hadn't been back since.

"Wait. Why?" someone asked.

"Because we're sick and tired of being victims."

"What do you want to accomplish?"

"Personally," the woman said, "I want to see what they have to say to a hundred angry women."

A laugh rose in my throat. These women weren't afraid of anything.

"I'm going," Stella whispered. "Are you?"

The group set off, chanting "Hey, hey, ho, ho—pornography has got to go!" We sounded like a pack of demented cheerleaders, and it felt good. We numbered about fifty but it seemed as if we were thousands stomping down Washington Street. We stopped in front of the Nasty Girl Bookstore. A husky, middle-aged man grinned at us through the plate-glass window. Our chant was angry: "Pornography has got to go!"

"F*** off," he mouthed to us.

Across the street, in front of the Pussy Cat Theatre, a woman in a halter-top and spandex skirt watched. She was smoking a cigarette and smiling. XXX, the marquee behind her read. LIVE SEX ACTS. "You go, girls," she shouted. "You just go."

Just then something clicked in my head—and I was ready. I was finally ready. The front door to the Nasty Girl Bookstore swung open. Fifty women piled in and crammed themselves between four narrow aisles. As I was propelled forward by the crush of the crowd, I thought in slow motion: *The Nasty Girl Magazine Shop for Perverts and Pigs.*

That's when a shelf of magazines came crashing to the floor. There was a whoop of joy as the unspoken message traveled through the shop: *We're going to close the Nasty Girl.* Another shelf was shoved over and two women jumped up and down on it. Magazines were ripped from their plastic sleeves and pieces of paper flew through the air. Bits of women's bodies—breasts, crotches, backsides—were torn, thrown, and trampled on. *I F***ed My Cousin,* one magazine was called. *Horny Coeds* was another. I surveyed the shelves and fixed my gaze on *Daddy's Little Girl.* On the front was a blond child, her hair in pigtails, an

199

oversized lollipop resting on her lips. She was fully made up and no more than five years old.

I clenched my teeth, tore the magazine in half, and tossed it into the air with the others.

I began to laugh, nervously. I had never done anything illegal before. Now, for sure, I was breaking the law and would have to pay. Perhaps my father was right—maybe I *would* go to jail for telling other people about what we did in secret.

There was a loud crash in the front of the store. I looked up to see the coach wielding a chair. She lifted it over her head and brought it down on top of a display case filled with handcuffs, hoods, and pacifiers shaped like little penises. For an instant, I felt pride.

"Look at this crap," she shouted, holding a fistful of pacifiers over her head.

Behind her, the shop owner, face twisted in anger, reached for a whip tacked to the wall.

"Watch out," I shouted, hearing my own voice echo in my chest.

The coach turned quickly and grabbed the whip. The two struggled, but she won. She reached into her pocket, pulled out a pocketknife, cut the whip in pieces and let it fall to the ground. The floor was already littered with penis pacifiers, and the crowd crushed them under their shoes. The handcuffs were then taken outside and dropped in the sewer. There. We were done at the Nasty Girl. Not a single magazine was salvageable. It had taken only five minutes.

Above the din, I heard sirens. "Split up," the coach yelled. "Go in different directions."

Stella and I began to run. "Wait a minute," she shouted as we turned the corner. "Stop or they'll know it was us." We stood together catching our breath, fighting the urge to bolt. My knees shook and my face was frozen in a grin.

"You liked that, didn't you?" Stella teased.

The next day Kevin turned up for breakfast. I felt exhilarated, and gestured wildly as I told about the coach, the chair, the racks of magazines. He listened quietly, then said: "I read the morning paper. It said you did thousands of dollars worth of damage."

I felt my jaw drop. "Yeah. To *pornography*. We did thousands of dollars of damage to pornography."

He wasn't impressed. "What do you think you accomplished by doing that?"

"I feel empowered," I said. "Like I'm not a victim anymore." My voice sounded high and tinny. I felt my eyes fill up. *Don't,* I told myself.

"Yeah, but you victimized someone else."

"No. I fought back."

"The paper's headline says *Feminism Breeds Violence*. Was that your goal?"

This time I met his stare. He seemed flat, colorless, and a vein was bulging on his forehead.

"You destroyed property, broke the law, and violated the First Amendment. Are you proud of that?"

The word *violate* rang in my ear. He was using it incorrectly. *Screw it,* I thought. *Judy can have him.* "I think you better go," I said.

That night I called Stella to see if she had seen the papers. She hadn't.

"It says there were a hundred of us," I told her.

She laughed. "The shop owner had to say that. He's probably embarrassed he couldn't handle fifty women."

"How do you feel now?" I asked. I could hear her breathing on the other end of the line. It sounded slow and steady. I wanted to be that calm. "Do you feel okay with what we did? Do you think we made a difference?"

"Well," she began, "it depends on what kind of difference you mean. If you mean, did we put a pornography shop out of business?—then no. They'll file an insurance claim and reopen in a week. But if you're talking personally—did that action make a personal difference to me?—then yes. It changed my world."

I sighed loudly. I felt relieved, as if a thick root had been pulled from my spine.

"It's not about destroying them," she continued. "It's about not letting them destroy you."

That night, images of my father bled into my dreams. The rage, the beatings. The way he stuttered, red-faced, as he whipped his belt from his pants. The choice was always the same—his belt or his dick. Either way, I usually got both.

The women from the rally were there, off to the side, reading my name over and over. My father was above me, hand raised in the air, belt wrapped tightly around his fist. Blood and fury gathered in his face. "You said my name," he roared.

I watched the arc of the leather strap as it cut through the air. But I was not afraid. I clenched my teeth and raised my arm to meet the belt. We struggled, but I took the belt from him. With a knife, I cut the belt in pieces and let it fall to the floor.

"You don't own me anymore," I told my father, my face pressed up against his. "You can't destroy me now."

He disappeared, evaporated into his own rage. And in my dream, I joined the women in the park.

elizabeth o'neill is a novelist and short-story writer who lives in the Northeast and now spends every Father's Day with her hubby and baby daughter, a very small but powerful feminist.

∞

No Screwing Around
vashti

I confronted him in the street yesterday, with neighbors looking on: "You've been screwing her since the week you got back, you insensitive bastard! *You have no respect for me.*"

True, meeting him for part of his tour through Europe had been a disaster, ending with us traveling in different directions and seemingly split. But I had written off the hellacious encounter as simply some weird travel dynamic. After all, he was one of my best friends. It was a friendship that had evolved so beautifully into a romantic relationship just a few months before our trip.

Now he started bumbling around for an excuse, so I continued, "You've been treating me like crap for weeks!"

"The thing with Sarah," he said, "just happened."

I slapped him across the face. "Another one of your pathetic excuses."

He jumped back. "That was uncalled for."

I walked right up to him. He looked nervous, even afraid. "You've been slapping me in the face over and over," I shouted. "You've been *spitting* in my face. You've been treating me like dirt, and you want to be my *friend?*" I spit on the ground. "Forget it!"

He got on his bike and started to leave. "I'm not going to sit around and—"

I interrupted and hollered, "I curse the memory of you in my life!"

Girl, I was yelling. Finally. It felt so good. I was just totally feeling, in my body, letting out everything that was all pent up, letting him hold and absorb the pain of two months of crying myself to sleep, transferring it from me to him, where it belonged.

I felt amazing afterward: so light, so free. I started laughing and dancing. When I turned around, I saw the three little girls from next door staring at me in wide-eyed wonder. I leaned over toward them, and said, "He deserved that." They got these huge grins on their faces and started giggling.

The next time they saw me, two minutes later, they were all excited and beaming up at me, cheering, "He deserved that!"

That made me happy.

vashti is a writer who don't take no guff. She is quite pleased to be a role model for little girls everywhere.

∞

Biker Babe
hilken mancini

I like to ride my bike because I can go anywhere at any time. This is important in Boston, where the public transit trains shut down at 12:30 A.M., or something ridiculous like that. Once, I found it was important in Boston for another reason, too.

Late one summer night, after some dumb loft party, I was heading home. I was twenty-two and living in a tiny apartment in the North End, Boston's historic Italian neighborhood. To get home, I often took a shortcut through Haymarket. By day it was packed with vendors and shoppers, and carts and tents filled with fruits, vegetables, and all kinds of smelly fish. At night the tents were empty. Only scraps of whatever wasn't sold that day would be left—tomatoes, cabbages, and onions strewn about the street. Traveling over the discarded tomatoes and old cobblestone roads, I could access an underpass—a little tunnel big enough for pedestrians and bikers, but not cars. Once through, I'd come out facing the North End, my neighborhood.

On that particular night, when I was almost at Haymarket, I slowed down to cut across traffic. There were only a few cars in the area at that hour and I kept pedaling, sure they knew to pass. Suddenly I got this creepy feeling that something was behind me: You know, when you can't tell if you're getting freaked out over nothing, or if something actually *is* about to happen, and then when it does, you feel dumb that you hadn't looked to see if your instinct had been right in the first place. Well, before I could turn around to check, I felt this hand—yes, a hand!—reach out and squeeze my ass.

Someone had grabbed my butt.

Before I knew it, I fell off my bike and onto the street. *Oww.* I looked up to see the offending car pick up speed and drive ahead. *Some jerk had knocked me off my bike to feel my ass,* was all I could think as I jumped back up. I couldn't let someone do that and get away with it. I pedaled to catch up. I didn't want to lose sight of the car. I was so angry I was shaking with rage. *What if there had been more cars behind me when I'd fallen?* I could easily have been hit.

I looked around as I pedaled and realized there was a traffic light ahead. I pedaled faster, thinking, *Turn red, turn red.* I gained speed and was now almost to the car. As I approached, I saw the scumbag guy in the passenger seat. Then I saw something that both freaked me out and bummed me out at the same time: There was a girl in the driver's seat. *Why would a girl do that to another girl?* The fact that she had slowed down just so some guy could pinch my ass was pathetic. My anger grew into a hateful disgust toward those two losers. *Screw them,* I growled as the traffic light changed from yellow to red. Their car slowed, then stopped. My heart was beating hard. I got closer, and from between my legs I pulled my kryptonite lock out of its holder. I lifted it as high as I could and brought it down hard before jerking my hand back. One fell swoop. The glass of their rear window sprayed into the backseat.

Knowing the underpass was just to my left, I darted across the street without even looking for cars. I was in that tunnel and under cover in a matter of seconds. I flew as fast as I could, even though I knew they couldn't catch me now unless they got out of their car to chase me. I was too scared to look back and check. Yeah, scared stiff . . . but exhilarated at the same time! I had never done anything like that before. When I reminded myself for the second time that there was no way they could have followed me, I relaxed and realized I was still gripping the kryptonite lock in my hand. I also realized that in my haste I hadn't looked to see the shock register on their faces when I had done my deed. One thing I'll bet though, the next time a guy asks that girl to slow down so he can squeeze some other girl's butt, she will think twice about whether or not she wants to replace another rear window.

hilken mancini (hmancini@vtiboston.com) works a boring day job as a librarian of film and video. By night she transforms into a kryptonite-lock-bearing-biker-superhero, as well as a songwriter/guitarist for the Boston rock band *Fuzzy* <www.baked.net/~vicster/fuzzy>.

∞

Driven
christine maxfield stone

My husband was having a voicemail romance. I found out one night when I heard him pick up the phone downstairs; I listened in on the upstairs extension. Their messages to each other were stupid and breathy, childish. At first I didn't know how to react to such a quirky sophomoric affair—but in the end, hell hath no fury like a woman scorned.

I got their mailbox number from the phone company's records. The "other woman" had unimaginatively used my husband's birth year as their pass code. I listened daily to their intimate little exchanges. I discovered they rarely saw each other; she lived nearly three hours away. He tended to call her when he was drinking and feeling lonely and rejected (which was every time he got drunk, because I wouldn't tolerate his sloppy, alcohol-impotent sexual advances).

The more I listened to their forlorn little soliloquies, the more my sense of betrayal was replaced by contempt at his poor taste and her gullibility and pitiful desperation. He sighed like a lovesick poet while she urged him to decisive action, suggesting he seize our pets and daughter (actually, *my* daughter from my previous marriage, although he neglected to tell her that part) and make a break for happiness-ever-after.

One day her message revealed her plan to come into the city for the night so they could rendezvous. It was on a day he and I had already arranged a late dinner together. So by midmorning he left a sappy, sad message telling her she'd have to cancel her plans; he couldn't be there.

I erased his message.

Come midafternoon she had left another message, telling him she needed to know of any problems right away because she would be leaving soon. Once again he left a response, a bit more urgent sounding, telling her not to come.

I erased that message, too.

That evening, just before my husband's quitting time, I went to the rendezvous point, a gas station parking lot, and waited. She soon pulled up in her beat-up station wagon. Emerging from my hiding spot behind the mini-mart, I quickly drove around front and pulled in close beside her so our drivers' windows were together and her car was pinned against the curb. I spoke with the graciousness and cordiality the occasion called for: "Bitch," I said, "it's time we talked."

She must have recognized me. She shook her head furiously, slammed down her car lock, and reached for her window knob.

"Wrong answer," I muttered, happy to move on to Phase II of my plans. I put my van in reverse, backed up about twenty feet, shifted into drive, and floored it. On impact, her door buckled, her window shattered, and she flew sideways into the passenger seat.

Time was standing still, the way it sometimes does when your system is splashing full of endorphins. I felt powerful but detached. I assessed my work as though I were an exacting demolition engineer. Not satisfied, I backed up and took aim again, this time for the car's rear end. *Crunch!* Her fender dug deep into the wheel well.

It occurred to me that in order to cause maximum grief I had to total her car. I backed up a third time and aimed for her front fender, battery, and radiator. The impact crumpled her hood like paper and flattened the front tire. By now she had escaped through the passenger door and was standing a few feet away, watching, shoulders hunched, clutching her arms to her chest.

"Now," I called to her matter-of-factly, "I'm gonna go get George, and we're gonna have a talk."

I drove the few blocks to my husband's job. He was just coming out, waving goodnight to friends, sauntering casually down the drive.

"We've got a little problem," I told him.

"What's wrong?"

"I just wrecked your whore's car up at the Gas 'n 'Go."

As we pulled back out onto the street, the police arrived—three cars with sirens screaming and lights flashing. We were ordered from our vehicle, hands above our heads. My husband had to lie on the ground as I was handcuffed. My van and purse were searched for weapons, drugs, and anything more interesting than the wife-and-mom crap they found there. As the police drove me away, my husband yelled "Don't worry, baby, I'll get you out. Don't worry!" at the back of the squad car.

What a drama queen.

He loved being part of the whole scene. In his mind, the incident served as proof of my devotion. For me, it was more about setting clear and unmistakable boundaries. My husband was oblivious to subtlety. He required grand statements. It wouldn't be enough to simply say, "No honey-humping on the side."

It worked. The affair ended, and my husband was extremely supportive and unflinching in court, in a twisted, charging-to-the-rescue sort of way.

But first I spent three days in jail awaiting arraignment. When I was finally brought to court, it became clear the system didn't have a standard procedure for anomalies like me. "Enjoy," a friend said. "It only happens once: the point at which you've done something truly rotten, but your record is clean as the driven snow."

I was originally charged with Felony Endangerment, but that was downgraded to Criminal Damage to Property. The DA and the judge acted embarrassed and apologetic for even giving me that. I looked like a hardworking mom, driving an old van, tending the garden, volunteering with her kid's youth group—oh, yeah, and in jail on criminal charges. I was Lucy, the Law-Abiding Citizen gone awry. This confused and upset them. Worse, I was reasonable and intelligent. At the very least, to make their decision-making easier, I should have been ranting and tearing at my hair.

I probably scared them, too. The police, attorneys, and judge knew I was a wronged wife. They likely concluded I'd been *driven* to this insane and desperate behavior by grief over my two-timing hubby. And who knows which of them had played with infidelity and were now fearful of being caught by their own sweet, cookie-baking, apron-wearing (knife-wielding?) wives. I made them nervous. *Fatal Attraction* nervous.

I suppose I *was* driven, like they thought, but the whole thing was a great deal more cold and rational than they guessed. I knew I would be caught, go to jail, *blah, blah, blah*. But the six hundred dollars I had to fork over in damages was a small price to pay for the satisfaction I got. The whole thing still feels magnificent, triumphant. I can see what career criminals get out of their work. What a rush!

christine maxfield stone is still driving the same Chevy van and the same husband in Milwaukee, Wisconsin. Putting her foot down (pedal to the metal) seems to have done the trick, and all honey-humping has remained intramarital. She cannot, however, vouch for any of the cops, attorneys, and judges in her county.

That Takes Ovaries! Open Mikes
(How cool is that?)

The work of a writer does not stop when her book is written. Today book promotions and author tours are an essential part of the job description. So while editing this book and strategizing for its (and my) future, I knew I'd have do the promotion dance, too. But instead of conducting a run-of-the-mill book tour where the author travels from city to city, sits in front of whoever she can draw to the bookstore, reads, and takes questions, I wanted to do something new, exciting—something different. Besides, I had to do something different; due to a physical disability, being on the road is difficult for me. My hope was to find some way to involve organizations and people at the grassroots level, raise funds and awareness for girls' issues and human rights, and at the same time limit my need to travel. Combined, these goals motivated me to imagine a completely innovative publicity and promotion strategy: I decided to tap into the main idea behind this book, the empowerment of people, and encourage women and girls to organize and speak out for themselves at each Ovaries event.

—Rivka

This book is important because of the voices in it—women and girls proudly shouting from the rooftops how they acted boldly in the world. Their stories are celebrations of womanly brazenness. But, *surprise!,* women and girls everywhere have triumphant stories to tell. So wouldn't it be exciting for the vibrant, feisty female voices in *your* community to be heard, too?

Enter the That Takes Ovaries! Open Mike.

There are two ways to make this happen. One is small, intimate, and held in your living room; suggestions for how to set this up are included below. The other is bigger, public, and held anywhere larger than your living room—a bookstore, coffee shop, university campus, poetry reading spot, auditorium. The guidelines for how to organize this second type of open mike are summarized below, with the full version found on the *That Takes Ovaries!* website <www.thattakesovaries.org>. Either event will give women and girls in your area an exhilarating chance to inspire and be inspired.

The topics can vary. General theme open mikes might draw the biggest crowds. Specific themes—sports, traveling, fighting back against racism or violence—might draw more dedicated, focused groups.

Whatever type of open mike you hold, it is modeled after this book. If you organize one, please support the book and its goals, and encourage people to take the message of empowerment home with them by having the paperback available (translation: for sale) at your event. Yes, this is a plug for the book—and for spreading the word about the audacious, outrageous, and courageous way we women and girls live our lives.

OVARIES IN YOUR LIVING ROOM

It's easy. Invite friends over, as you would for any other party, and tell them to bring their friends, too—new blood makes things more fun. If you want, use this e-mail invitation (shaded box) that the book editor (that's me!) sent out when she held her own Living Room Open Mike.

Before your Living Room Open Mike, please contact the book website simply to indicate you are hosting one. This is encouraged, not required. It just helps me to know where and how many living-room soirees are being held. If you'd like to support the book and have it available to sell at your event you

Please join [your name] for a way cool
THAT TAKES OVARIES!™ Living Room Open Mike

Come tell & hear real-life stories about being a brazen babe. Stories can cover anything YOU have *ever* done—little or big—that was bold, gutsy, outrageous, audacious, courageous, or inspirational. It can be playful, serious, spontaneous, calculated, smart, sexy, and/or an example of leadership. It could be an act that defies racism/sexism/ableism/classism & homophobia . . . or not. Anything that when you think about it today, makes you nod your head with *pride* or even semi-disbelief and think, *"Wow! I did that!"*

Stories should be true and short, 1–7 minutes. (Helpful to time your story aloud beforehand.) Come ready to read your written story—or share one off the top of your head.

DATE/TIME: Anyday, Anytime

PLACE: (Your name)'s cozy, hopefully crowded, living room

ADDRESS: Anystreet, Anytown, Anycountry

DIRECTIONS: Take a right, then a left, blah, blah, blah

QUESTIONS & RSVP: Call (Your name, phone, e-mail)

COST: Free (Or collect donations for some good causes!) (See below)

WHO: All ages/genders invited

(Optional lingo: Guys, come share stories about moms, sisters, and daughters.)

Male-bashing, and Why It Won't Be Helpful At Your *Ovaries!* Event

Yes, we still live in a patriarchal society. Yes, the majority of people who hurt (harass, abuse, rape, murder) women and girls are men. For this reason, some stories heard at your event may be about how women and girls fought back. These stories are important; we need to tell them, people need to hear them. But if we want things to change—truly, radically change—we need to understand the full complexity of how a society steeped in sexism hurts *all* involved. How it tries to turn inherently strong girls into women who hesitate to use their power, and inherently compassionate boys into men with an inclination to dominate or hurt. For any one group to be free of these harmful effects of institutionalized sexism, we *all* need access to our full range of emotions and abilities; we *all* need to escape the gender roles and rules our culture declares definitive.

There are many tactics we can use to achieve this goal. Some include anger. Anger is often an appropriate response to being hurt and sometimes a necessary first step to reclaiming one's power (and ability to fight back against assault). But it won't be helpful to direct anger at men who attend your open mike. They came to support women. Besides, if our ultimate goal is to "reach" someone, change their heart and mind, then anger, and certainly bashing, will likely trigger their defense mechanisms. And then those we'd specifically hoped would learn and grow can't even hear how their attitude and behavior affect us.

Happily, there are other tactics we can employ: education, guidance, perspective sharing, and simply telling the truth about our lives. Hearing the truth, for the first time or the hundredth time, can be transformational. Given that, set a tone at your open mike where the truth about how women and girls have been hurt and how they fought back can be told, without simultaneously asserting that *all* men participate in the hurting. If needed, remind your audience that good men have always stood side by side with women in our mutual struggles to be free.

May your *Ovaries!* event be made up of the transformative stuff that tears down walls, not raises them. Good luck!

have options: One, buy a bunch of copies from a bookstore (go local, go independent!), recoup costs when you sell them at your party, and return the ones you don't sell. Check the store's return policy first, and *save that sales receipt*. Bookstores are the best way to go, but if you simply can't make arrangements with one, you can order books directly from Random House special sales at 1-800-729-2960. Your event, Ms. Hostess, will rouse women and girls to raise their voices and will give them a chance to look at their own lives and identify their courage; taking the book home will keep them inspired long after the evening has ended.

When at last your living room is brimming with people, here's what I suggest: Bring out the chips and dip, read aloud the book's preface, called "Rivka's Note to All Readers" (which sets the tone), plus a couple of stories (which model the storytelling style), then go around the room and have everyone share her (or his) own true stories. It is a homey, sofa-pillows type of comfortable, and it's entertaining and inspirational—all rolled into one. Feel free to use any activities from the *At the Event Itself* section detailed in the Open Mike Guidelines found on the website. Make sure everyone who wants to speak gets a chance. Tell folks in advance to keep their stories short: maybe one to seven minutes? You don't want any one person hogging the floor (oink, oink). If someone does, don't be shy: Interrupt and announce her allotted time is about up. Then make sure it is. Being a Benign Dictator is easier than you might think. Or use an oven timer, the Instrument of Neutral Democracy.

It's a girl thing, so likely not a lot of guys will come. If some do, make them feel welcome (we can always use good men in the revolution, and at parties) and remind them that they can tell stories about the ovaries in their lives—female friends and family members. Some actually might, and then you are in for a treat; it is a treasure to hear men appreciate women's boldness.

Before anyone leaves, tell your girl-guests that if they want their stories considered for any subsequent *Ovaries!* books they should check the website for submission info.

ORGANIZING A (BIGGER, PUBLIC) *THAT TAKES OVARIES!* OPEN MIKE

If you want to have more than just a few friends over; if you want to see strangers (who are only friends you have not yet met) excitedly milling around, talking about doing audacious things; if you want to bring women and girls together to listen, clap, and cheer with huge grins on their faces; if you want to feel powerful, smart, and in charge, like *you* can plan and pull off a great time for lots of folks—and raise their consciousness to boot—then you want to organize a bigger, public *That Takes Ovaries!* Open Mike. Good for you.

Luckily for everyone, the book's control-freaky editor cannot be involved with most events. So instead, there are guidelines for open mike organizers, like you, to use. The guidelines are summarized below, with the full version found on the website.

What? You say you have never organized a public event before?

Well, hey, now's your chance. You never know, this might start your new career in organizing for women's empowerment. Or it could just be a lot of fun—once.

You can work as an individual, or under the auspices of an established organization. You can hold a stand-alone event, or

216

include the open mike as a fun, audience participatory component to an already-scheduled larger conference (big advantages: comes with a site and pre-made audience). Or you can hold it in a bookstore. Options galore! Be creative.

Unlike a smaller Living Room Open Mike, where I have suggestions but no requirements, if you want to organize a bigger, public open mike, you will have to do Certain Things. I list them here. But first, a definition of what exactly a "bigger, public" *That Takes Ovaries!* Open Mike is. It is any gathering that uses "That Takes Ovaries!" or any like-wording in its promotion and: (1) is open to the public or local community—such as your city, neighborhood, or school; (2) includes more than just your friends and your friends' friends; (3) is publicized, perhaps with a publicly posted flyer or listing in a newspaper, school, or community events calendar; and/or (4) may be covered by the media. Lastly, if you expect more than thirty people, whoever they are, consider your open mike "bigger, public."

FUND-RAISER, TOO!

In keeping with the philosophy that it is important to give back to our communities, I encourage each (bigger, public) open mike organizer to make her event a fund-raiser, and to split the proceeds between two causes: one local, one international. We females are scattered far and wide; by dividing up our resources locally and internationally, we cover all bases.

Some of the money collected can go to covering costs (though it is hoped that sponsors or in-kind donations will take care of that), and, if necessary, to paying the organizer something. But regardless of costs, most of the proceeds should go to the beneficiaries of the fund-raiser.

It is my suggestion and hope that a portion of the money raised go to a local girls' program—whichever one you like in your community. (If you need an idea, consider your nearest chapter of Girls Inc. (www.girlsinc.org), one of the nation's preeminent girls' organizations. They help girls with everything

**So the open mike you want to organize meets
the above "bigger, public" definition?
And now you are wondering,
"What are these *Certain Things* I'll have to do?"**

Thing 1. On the website, register your intention to organize an open mike. (This is simple. Don't let having to do it be a hindrance.)

Thing 2. The complete, not just summarized, *Guidelines for Organizing an Open Mike* are found on the website. When you register, you agree to follow the complete guidelines. As you read them, you will see they are fairly flexible. You can alter and adapt them to your specific community's needs.

Thing 3. Wait to hear back from the website before beginning to organize.

There are good reasons for Things 1–3. I need to coordinate and keep track of what is going on around the country. We wouldn't want two open mikes in the same city on the same week, now would we? Also, if you want, we can electronically list your upcoming event for all to see—and attend. Besides, contact with the website means you'll have someone who cares as much as you do about the event. And someone to whom you can brag when it goes swimmingly.

from self-defense to economic empowerment to preventing adolescent pregnancy.) If you search high and low but cannot find a local girls' group that seems right for an *Ovaries!* fundraiser, pick a women's group.

It is my further hope that another portion of the money your event raises will be dedicated to stopping two of the most appalling international human rights abuses perpetrated against women and girls—sexual enslavement and, separately, female genital mutilation (FGM) (for info on these two horrific violations of girls' rights and sexual freedom, see page 223). To this end, *That Takes Ovaries!* established a relationship with Equality Now (www.equalitynow.org), a New York–based international women's organization that, among other things, works with grassroots groups around the globe to eradicate FGM as well as the sex trafficking of girls. Some of the writers in this book have already generously donated their contributor's honorarium to Equality Now. Imagine if every open mike distributed information and made a donation, too. We could make a real difference in the crucial goal of educating the public and ending both sexual slavery and FGM. And we would be sending a strong message that women in the so-called First World, a world of privilege, care about all women around the globe. (Note: If there is another international women's cause you'd prefer to donate to, that is also an option. Donating to Equality Now is strongly encouraged but not required.)

For those of you who have never organized for a cause or never before seen yourselves as social change activists— Welcome! Please use this event to get your feet (and knees and

Multi-Culti is Good

Have your event reflect the diversity around you. Invite, leaflet, and advertise in a variety of cultural communities. Be imaginative. Reach out to Asian resource centers, Black sororities, disability rights groups, battered women's shelters, gay/straight alliances, girls' associations, Latino advocacy centers, Native American youth groups, LGBT listservs, senior citizen programs, and the like. Encourage women and girls from various backgrounds to take the lead as organizers, publicists, emcees. Diversity makes us stronger. Coalitions make us more effective.

tush) wet. There is nothing like the high that comes from making a difference.

PRE-EVENT ORGANIZING CHECKLIST

• Register your intention to organize a (bigger, public) *That Takes Ovaries!* Open Mike. Wait until you hear back before proceeding further.

• Prepare yourself for a bunch of fun and a good bit of work: Depending on how big you want it to be, the event could take one to three months to pull off.

• Find a coorganizer or loyal servants, umm, assistants, who will help.

• Find a free/absurdly cheap, wheelchair accessible, close-to-public-transit site. Try a bookstore, coffee shop, university campus, poetry reading spot, club, auditorium, beauty parlor waiting room, bowling alley parking lot, whatever. (Or piggyback onto another organization's already scheduled conference. Its organizers might love an audience participatory activity. And this way your site and crowd are already secured. Yippee!)

• Invite local girls' and women's organizations to join the fun by having them coorganize, sponsor, publicize, and/or attend the event.

• Consider inviting local celebrities and leaders. They will bring their fans, and can read from the book, tell their own personal stories, or emcee. Which gets us to . . .

• Secure a Mistress of Ceremonies (emcee). She should be vibrant and bold (like the book!), and, most important, able to make crowds comfortable enough to share personal stories aloud. *Maybe she is you?*

- If you are not already holding the open mike at a bookstore, invite the owner or manager of one to attend your event to sell the book. This helps promote the paperback—thank you!—and further legitimizes your open mike by linking it to the book. (P.S. Don't forget to support your local *independent* bookstores.)

- Schedule an up-to-two-hour agenda. Choose activities from the *At the Event Itself* options (summarized below; full version found on the website).

PRE-EVENT PUBLICITY CHECKLIST

- Get a nifty *Ovaries!* publicity packet off the website.
- Make an eye-catching (hot pink?) hardcopy flyer about the event, and an e-mail flyer, too.
- E-mail and snailmail flyers to all potentially interested individuals and groups, like local women's centers, YWCA, N.O.W., Girls Inc., and Girl Scouts chapters.
- Pass out flyers at poetry slams, clubs, knitting conventions, pro-choice demos, and any public gathering of one or more people. Post on windows and community bulletin boards in libraries, bookstores, coffee shops, beauty salons, gynecologists' offices—anywhere you'd find women chillin'.
- Get the open mike listed in the calendar section of local publications.
- If you want more publicity, like your fifteen seconds of fame, contact local TV stations and city newspapers' entertainment/around town/style reporters and book reviewers. Their interests will be piqued by a *That Takes Ovaries!* Open Mike. It's playful *and* depthful, and it has just enough "edge" to draw them in.

AT THE EVENT ITSELF

Activities you can use at your event are listed in the Open Mike Guidelines on the website. Pick the ones you think would work best with the community you are inviting. A bare-bones open mike consists of only three components: first, the *Introduction,* when the Mistress of Ceremonies reads aloud the book's preface (aka "Rivka's Note to All Readers") and discusses the importance of women and girls publicly sharing their brazen, outrageous, audacious, courageous acts; second, *Modeling the Storytelling Style,* when someone role-models the types of stories we hope to hear at the event (i.e. true, short, and, of course, gutsy), perhaps by reading aloud examples from the book; and last, the actual *Open Mike Time,* when women and girls who came with a story already prepared share them with the whole room, thereby motivating others to spontaneously share stories, too. With just those three components, you will have a great event!

However, other activities can also be found on the website, such as *Celebrity Readings,* when well-known, crowd-drawing locals tell stories from their own lives or read from the book; the *Golden Ovaries Award Ceremony,* when community-based women and girls who have acted boldly are honored and then tell their specific act of brazenness to the audience; the *Greater Audience Involvement* exercise, when all who attend have a chance to share their stories in a small group setting, and then later, if they want, with the whole room. The exercise is a fun way to help bring shy people out and build their self-esteem.

No matter how you proceed with your open mike, the clapping, cheering, supportive yelps and congratulatory pats on the back at the end of every story will encourage each woman and girl to keep being gutsy, keep taking risks in her day-to-day life. And when the electrified crowd finally dances its way out the door, you can be sure they'll know that being *Women With Ovaries* enhances their own lives and serves as a fine example to others of what a woman can be.

Female Genital Mutilation, Sex Trafficking, and That Takes Ovaries! Fund-raisers

It is my hope that the *That Takes Ovaries!* Open Mikes that you organize (especially the bigger, public ones) will be fund-raisers, with a percentage of the money raised going to local girls' groups and a percentage going to the organization Equality Now for their work to stop female genital mutilation (FGM) and the equally horrible but separate atrocity of sexual enslavement. (For general info on fund-raising, see page 218.)

FGM is one of the most atrocious human rights abuses perpetrated against girls around the globe. To date, 130 million females from Africa to Europe and the United States have been mutilated and suffer permanent disabilities from the barbaric act. An unknown number die each year during and after the procedure. Equality Now works with community-based leaders and grassroots groups worldwide to promote a better understanding of FGM and effective strategies for its eradication

This is how Fauziya Kassindja, who managed to escape FGM, describes it in her story in *That Takes Ovaries!*:

A harmful traditional practice among some African, Asian, and Middle Eastern cultures, female genital mutilation (FGM) is performed on about two million infants, girls, and women each year. That's more than five thousand a day. Depending on the local custom, you will either "only" have your clitoris cut off, or you will lose the whole thing, including labia minora and majora. If it is the latter, you are sewn up, leaving a small hole, hardly big enough to allow pee and menstrual blood to squeeze out. Then, with each baby you birth, you are recut and resewn anew. The rationale behind FGM is complex: It is tradition; it is thought to protect virginity and prevent promiscuity; uncircumcised females are considered dirty; girls must be cut as a requirement for marriage; and circumsised girls and women are deemed more sexually desirable.

The practice of FGM subjects women to a number of long-term physical and psychological problems. Often carried out without anesthesia and with unsterilized razors or knives, it is a sometimes deadly practice. My other aunt died from it, as do many girls every year, either from hemorrhaging or infection.

I wanted nothing to do with either the [forced] marriage or the so-called circumcision, so with the help of my sister, and my mother from afar, I fled that very day.

Fauziya left her home, her family, her country to escape the brutality of FGM. Today, in part because of her work publicizing the horrors of FGM, Fauziya's homeland of Togo, West Africa, has outlawed the practice. But it still goes on legally and illegally around the world. Equality Now is one of the leading organizations working to stop it.

They also work to end global sex trafficking of girls and women. Ruchira Gupta describes sexual slavery in India in her story in *That Takes Ovaries!*:

I came to learn that the sale of girls is no secret; it is all done in the open, like any business. There is the local procurer, an uncle or fellow villager, who buys the girl from her parents for twenty to thirty dollars. He'll collect three or four females, aged seven to thirty, bring them to a bigger town, collect another dozen girls from other rural areas, put them all in a truck, smuggle them over the Nepal-India border (where he'll pay off the border police), then sell them to the next middleman up the chain, in India. The new men take the girls to small boardinghouses. There they rape the girls, beat them, subjugate their spirits completely until they do whatever these men want. The men sometimes use ice to break in the premenstrual girls. Then the girls are taken to Bombay and sold to brothel madams for three thousand rupees apiece, about forty to fifty dollars.

Back in Bombay, I heard how the half-grown children are bonded sex slaves for the first five years, unpaid and forced to "service" twenty-five to thirty men a day: *raped* twenty-five to thirty times a day! "Clients" stub out cigarettes on their young breasts and shove bottles up their vaginas. They are kept in five-by-seven-foot rooms each crammed with about four miniature beds. The rooms have no walking space, just beds and curtains separating them. Windows are barred, entrances locked and guarded. A severe beating follows any attempt to flee. After five years, they are allowed to keep half their meager earnings. By then the madams have made sure that the girls have become addicted to drugs and alcohol and have had a baby, so they won't run. The girls, now with distorted, almost caricatured bodies, get trapped by disease and debt—they have to pay for water, bedding, and food. By age forty they are usually dead from AIDS.

I learned that this horror goes on around the globe, from Africa to Albania. Each year 4 million girls are sold by their impoverished parents, tricked with false promises of good jobs, or outright kidnapped. They are brought to big cities in their own country or sent abroad to rich Western nations. Fifty thousand are shipped to the United States each year.

Both Ruchira's and Fauziya's descriptions help to explain why *That Takes Ovaries!* established a relationship with Equality Now and why I strongly suggest you send them a percentage of the money raised at any *Ovaries!* Open Mikes.

Equality Now
P.O. Box 20646
Columbus Circle Station
New York, NY 10023
Phone: (212) 586-0906
Fax: (212) 586-1611
E-mail: info@equalitynow.org
Website: www.equalitynow.org

Acknowledgments
¡Mega-muchas gracias!

To three heroines:

HARRIET TUBMAN, who, despite the threat of lynching, escaped—and then went back again and again to guide fellow Africans from the horrors of slavery via the Underground Railroad.

WONDER WOMAN, who gave girls starved for positive images of our own a way to envision ourselves as wielders of great physical power and agents of world change.

BELLA ABZUG, a smart, tenacious, loud, and proud fighter—champion!—of women's social, political, and economic rights. My first feminist role model (after my parents, of course).

∞

It should be made part of our common knowledge, told to every newborn upon making it out the canal: "Welcome to the world, baby! Oh, and FYI, the Earth is round, mufflers are made to rot just after the warranty runs out, and it's a ton and a half of work to compile an anthology." That way would-be writers will know in advance and can thus choose to channel their overachiever energies in other arenas, like, say, *anything else.* Complaints aside, I loved working on this book. And it couldn't have happened without these folks:

The Decades-Long Inner Circle: A big thanks to these people, my "core group," for E•V•E•R•Y•T•H•I•N•G—from seemingly unconditional love to dollops of emotional (and financial!) support, for teaching me how to act decisively, courageously, compassionately. To Mom & Dad: I love you. I am so lucky and grateful to have you. All the gutsy things I ever do in my life come from having watched you do it first. To my sister: In our quest to save the world, we split it fifty-fifty—she got the natural earth, I got its human inhabitants. I've fallen short, but she's doing an amazing job. Thanks for encouragement and for modeling how to be an effective leader. To my auntie for her warmth, affection, generosity, and our shared struggles. To my uncle for caring about family. To the indispensable trio: Patsy, Jevera, and Mireya (my angel on Earth, thank you for standing by me for so long).

Lucky me, I've had a posse of wonderful writing assistants—all energetic, colorful, caring, and smart. Without their help editing, writing, and typing, *That Takes Ovaries!* would have remained a mere book proposal. In order of appearance these Supergirls are: Jessica Turco, the let's-face-it-she's-invaluable Julia Magnusson, Alisa Moskowitz, Janna Weinstein, Shauna Rogan, Sarah Tyler.

A special *"Oy,* am I glad you exist," to Ellen Samuels, who skillfully edited some of these stories, and gives this writer a fab friendship based on support and perennially useful advice. Warm hugs to Richard Hoffman and England's Crown Jewels, Joan and Louie Solomon, for helping me recognize I had a career in writing. For the combo of friendship, editing, and sharp thinking: B*o*b*b*i, Hanne Blank, Marie Celestin, Hannah Doress, Jan Gardner, the irrepressible Loolwa Khazzoom, Tommye-K Mayer, Peggy Munson, Elizabeth O'Neill, Martha Ramsey, Susan and Mimi Parker, Katie Wheeler, and the dedicated and generous Gail Dines, the one person besides my editor who graciously commented on near every story and intro in the manuscript. For being my buddies and assisting with many computing and artistic tasks: Will

Ballard, Lee Mandell, Vicki Van Sant. To friends who make my life more depthful and playful: Ami & Holli, John Grebe, essential-to-my-health John Herd, Peter ("the cape's at the cleaners") Kane, tenacious Judy Krugerwoman, David Levy, Joan Livingston, Rosie and Theresa McMahan, Eva y Roberto, Susan Mortimer, geekboy-on-wheels Michael Muehe, Jean Perrin, One Angry Girl Jill Portugal, Frezzia y Yessenia y Gabriel, Eli Rosenblatt, Mistress of Hedonism Meg Rosser, Jan Sunoo, the guys at Superior, Jose Luis Sandoz, Adam T-Zak, Cecelia Wambach.

For offering comments, or help with networking and writing, I thank Cathy Armer, Joani Blank, Soul Brown, Kari Bodnarchuk, Teresa Dovidio, Ophira Edut, Holly Jackson, Patricia A. Johnson, Shoshanna Kaplinsky, Julayka Latigua, Lynn Lu, Kathy Morris, Regina Preciado (Benevolent Dictator of the Writergrrls), Amy Richards, Liz Skipper, Naomi Sweitzer, Kara Trott, Theresa Urist, Janie Ward, and all the Writergrrls. Thanks to Siobhán Ohmart <E-gateco.com> for initial website development and Martha Friend for photography.

The National Writers Union is vital—necessary if we want to organize for our rights as writers. Join today <www.nwu.org>! Involved in this book were the generous NWU Contract Advisors Lee Lockwood and Phil Mattera, and NWU Goddess Barbara Beckwith. Vital to other legal aspects is Steve, trademark attorney with a heart of gold.

My Repetitive Strain Injury team is made up of these mensches and miracle workers who keep me able to work: the Coalition for New Office Technology, Rick Bird, Jenn Dean, Peggy Dellea, Priscilla Mann, Diane Sheehan.

A decade and a half of thanks to Doc Hubbuch.

My deep appreciation to everyone dedicated to finding the cause and cure for Chronic Fatigue Immune Dysfunction Syndrome (CFIDS), for all the research, advocacy, and info dissemination you have done, and all the patient care and support you have given. Living with unrelenting exhaustion, brain-fog-as-thick-as-pea-soup, and the societal stigmatization of this invisible and poorly named but very real and debilitating physical illness, is . . . well, hard. Anyone who lives in spite of CFIDS's life-altering restrictions has BIG ovaries. For info: CFIDS Association of America, P.O. Box 220398, Charlotte, NC 28222-0398, USA; (800) 442-3437; (704) 365-2343; www.cfids.org

Thanks to Eileen Cope, Barbara Lowenstein, and the crew at Lowenstein Associates for agenting my book beyond the call of duty. Thanks to Rachel Kahan, my editor at Random House, who immediately understood the book's message and goal, and whose support was/is sooooo helpful.

My heartfelt appreciation to the hundreds of women and girls who submitted their stories for this book, including those who did and did not make the final cut.* You are amazing! You have plowed through oppression, sailed gracefully around obstacles, jumped over barriers, and walked through fear. Whether you impulsively did something sorta silly, or wisely implemented a well-thought-out altruistic deed, in the end you playfully danced on top of dead, outdated stereotypes, and therefore blazed new trails for the rest of us to follow. *Go get 'em, grrrrrrrrls!*

---

*Adrienne, Krissy, and Rachel: After you submitted your stories and I chose to include them in the book, I searched high and low for you but you had disappeared. Please contact me and we'll give you proper credit in any subsequent editions.—Rivka

About the Author

Author photograph: David Levy.
T-shirt courtesy of www.oneangrygirl.net

RIVKA SOLOMON writes and rabble-rouses on the East Coast. Her work has appeared in national magazines, newspapers, and anthologies and has aired on radio broadcasts—including all the right places, such as *Bitch: Feminist Response to Pop Culture; Bust: The New Girl Order; Lilith Magazine; MoXi: For the Woman Who Dares; Sojourner: The Women's Forum;* and *WBUR,* Boston's National Public Radio news station. Since damn near babyhood, she has been a women's rights advocate and activist.

progressive, AGGRESSIVE, aggressive, pushy

unstoppable, uncontrollable, overwhelming, zestfu

spirited, lively, effervescent, heady, dynamic, dynamite

passionate, passion for life, dashing, sharp, snappy

insistent, pressing, driving, valorous, gallant, heroine

Amazonian, tough, **MACHA,** militant, fierce

venturesome, enterprising, mettlesome, high-spirited

high-souled, high-hearted, proudhearted, stouthearted

brave-hearted, firm-minded, strong-minded, unswayed

firm, STEADY, dogged, indomitable, never sa

die, persevering, determined, resolute, of high morale

sporting, ready for danger, ready for the fray, ready f

anything, Thelma and Louise-ish, **unflinching**

unshrinking, leading the charge, willing, free-and-eas

carefree, unforeseeing, not looking, incautious, unwar

heedless. uncalculating, frivolous, devil-ma

care, mischievous, slaphappy, unpredictable, reckles

damning the consequences, wanton, wild, wild ar

razy, impetuous, throw caution to the wind, abandon

ommon sense, cavalier, **OVERDARING,**

verbold, madcap, daredevil, all-or-nothing, do-or-die,

reakneck, danger-loving, thrill-seeking, risk-taking,

eath-defying, overambitious, over-the-top, oversure,

verconfident, rash, ill-conceived, ill-advised,

arebrained, foolhardy, wildcat, indiscreet, imprudent,

it-or-miss, presumptuous, optimistic, hell-bent, raising

ell, unchecked, headstrong, wicked, willful, excitable,

npatient, ***hot-blooded,*** fire-eating, furious,

ockeyed, cockamamie, silly, foolish, unguarded,

oontaneous, hasty, impulsive, flaunting, unflappable,

xorbitant, extreme, extravagant, utmost, surpassing,

xceeding, exaggerated, *over the limit,* beyond

e pale, huge, oversized, overabundant, surpassing,

reposterous, gritty, outlandish, true grit, backbone,

AVING HEART, having courage, having moxie, screw

o one's courage, walk through fear...having ovaries!